The Superpowers
and Regional
Tensions

The Superpowers and Regional Tensions

The USSR, the United States, and Europe

William E. Griffith
Massachusetts Institute of
Technology

LexingtonBooks
D.C. Heath and Company
Lexington, Massachusetts
Toronto

Library of Congress Cataloging in Publication Data

Griffith, William E.
    The superpowers and regional tensions.

    Includes index.
    1. World politics—1975–1985. 2. Soviet Union—Foreign relations—
1975–   . 3. United States—Foreign relations—1981–   . 4. Europe—
Foreign relations—1945–   . 5. Détente. 6. Arms control. I. Title.
D849.G72   327'.0904   81–47649
ISBN 0–669–04702–3   AACR2

Published simultaneously in Canada

Printed in the United States of America

International Standard Book Number: 0–669–04702–3

Library of Congress Catalog Card Number: 81–47649

Contents

Preface

This book tries to analyze the interaction between Soviet-U.S. bilateral relations and European problems. I hope to follow it with another on Soviet-U.S. relations and the Middle East.

I have incurred many debts of gratitude during its writing. I am most of all grateful to *The Reader's Digest* and to its editor-in-chief, Edward T. Thompson, for sponsoring many summer trips which enabled me to study European problems on the spot. I am also grateful for research support to the Earhart Foundation and its president, Richard Ware. My secretary, Meri Whitaker, and my typist, Nancy Hearst, helped me to put the manuscript in a form fit to publish. I am particularly grateful to my former research assistant, John Van Oudenaren, with whom I have discussed most of this book and from whose comments I have greatly profited. But I alone am responsible for what the reader will find here.

1

The Decline of Détente and Arms Control and Implications for Europe

Europe was the main theater of the first cold war. The Middle East and South-east Asia seemed likely, in mid-1981, to become the main theater of the second one. In 1981 Europe was so weak, the USSR was so strong, nuclear weapons threatened such unestimable destruction, and Europe had become so dependent on oil from the Persian Gulf that the Eastern Question which plagued London, Paris, Berlin, Vienna, and St. Petersburg during the whole nineteenth century, had become more dangerous for Europe and for détente than it ever had before.

Simultaneously, the Soviet military buildup and political expansionism, the technological leap forward of weapons systems, and rising conservatism in the United States and in the USSR weakened détente and changed U.S. priorities from arms control to arms buildup, while Western Europe was determined to remain an island of détente, something which Brezhnev, for his own reasons, wanted it to be but about which Reagan, for his own reasons, was notably, if not publicly, less enthusiastic.

In 1981, Western Europe was trying to reassert its foreign policy autonomy from Washington. Poland was trying to reassert its domestic autonomy from Moscow. Washington was thus disturbed, and the Soviet Empire threatened, in their most strategic areas.

Although Western Europe's power and Poland's determination were greater than ever since 1945, they were both still affected by the superpowers' military buildups and by European military weakness in the Persian Gulf, on which Western Europe's economies depended. Thus, before turning to Europe's problems and their interaction with the superpowers, let us first consider the background of the superpowers themselves and their relations with each other.

The USSR

The traditional passivity of the Russian people and the normal ruthlessness of their rulers have so far prevented Soviet problems from endangering Soviet stability. In this respect, the Bolshevik Revolution may turn out to have been at least as much an interlude as a turning point. By 1981 the Soviet elite ruled its people no longer primarily by revolutionary ideology. It had become instead profoundly conservative, bureaucratic, and Great Russian nationalist.[1]

By 1981, the USSR was a party-state gripped by the peaceful transition to feudalism. Its privileged communist stratum was an estate that increasingly

1

perpetuated itself by inheritance. Like feudal lords, its elite did not own property in fee simple, but instead they owned privileges and often passed them on to their children. Those who did not belong to the ruling class were better than, but not that much better than, serfs. Dissidents, like heretics, were repressed, but party members, like feudal nobles, usually were not.

This analogy, like all others, is also misleading. By 1981 the Soviet elite was also modernized, bureaucratized, and secularized—that is, unquestioned belief in Marxism-Leninism had given way to the professional and administrative ethos and Great Russian nationalism. The alienation and repression that as a result arose, in a part of the masses, and in a small minority of the elite, gave rise, as it did in Iran, to the revival of religion, primarily the Russian Orthodox church. Alcoholism at least as much dissolved alienation as it did in the gin mills of eighteenth-century London. The memory of Stalin's repression and the post-Stalin rise in living standards had until recently made the Soviet people expect further improvement of their lot. By early 1981, however, disillusion had set in. Hope was giving way to the erosion of civil morale and morality, at least among urban Great Russians. New social problems had come home to roost. They had largely arisen out of the disappointment which followed on this earlier revolution of rising expectations. By 1981, the USSR was very different than it had been in the 1950s. Consumerism, cynicism, influence of and ties with the West had spurred appetites—and discontents.

Russians have always been heavy drinkers, but by 1981 alcoholism had become a plague. Male death rates had increased, rarely in developed states, primarily because of alcoholism. Infant mortality also increased, equally rarely in developed states, because of abortions and bad medical care. Other aspects of Soviet life, more impressionistic and difficult to measure, also worsened, as did their hopes for the future. Economic growth declined to around 2 percent. There was no reason to believe that it would markedly revive. Traditional, recurrent bad weather plus continued low productivity of collective farms required massive grain imports.

Future Soviet prospects were worse. A labor shortage loomed, particularly of skilled labor and investment capital. Investment capital would have to come from European Russia, but the only labor surplus would increasingly be among Muslims in Soviet Central Asia, whose birth rate by 1981 was five times that of the Great Russians. Since few Muslims were likely to move to European Russia, new factories would have to be brought to them. By 2000, around one-third of recruits to the Red Army are expected to be Muslims—unskilled, largely not Russian speaking, and perhaps by then susceptible to rising Islamic fundamentalism.

In theory, these problems required drastic economic reforms. However, such reforms were not likely (nor was a return to the bloodier aspects of Stalinism) for they would threaten the power and privileges of the communist elite. The traditional passivity of the Soviet population and the intelligentsia's fear of liberalization's resulting in anarchic outbursts of the black people, plus omnipresent KGB repression, made reforms unlikely. Moreover, by 1981 the small, harassed, almost decimated groups of Great Russian dissidents had only liberalization, but not Great Russian nationalism, on their side. They thus could not hope to win a Great Russian mass base. Nor was the approaching generational change in the Soviet leadership—for that was what it inexorably would be—likely to produce radical reforms. On the contrary, exactly its bureaucratic character, its probable factionalization after Brezhnev's departure before a new leader would win out, and its temptation to fly into foreign policy would probably make the new leadership go on muddling through.

The situation among the other nations of the USSR—for they are nations, not "nationalities" as Moscow likes to call them—was different, especially among those with long, proud historic traditions, such as the Baltic states, Georgia, and the Ukraine, for there nationalism and religion united to favor liberalization. Dissent was, for example in Lithuania, mass based. This inevitably stimulated nationalism among the Great Russians, however, just as it had under the tsars, and it made them believe Moscow's arguments against liberalization, especially among the other Soviet nations—that is, if the USSR were threatened by Sino-U.S. encirclement, as Great Russians increasingly feared, how could it hold together if its other nations were allowed self-determination? It was exactly *because* the USSR is the last great colonial empire that the end of Great Russian domination of the other Soviet nations would mean the end of the USSR as a superpower. Thus for Russia, as always, empire meant being a great power, and decolonization meant not only the end of the empire but also the threat of Soviet subjugation to hostile foreign powers. As Brezhnev said in 1968 to the Czechoslovak Politburo when he dragged them to Moscow after he had invaded their country, the USSR is determined to keep control over all the territory it won in World War II at the cost of so much blood, sweat, and tears.[2] How much more is Great Russian leadership determined not to allow the USSR to break up?

Soviet Foreign Policy

Soviet foreign policy, like any other major power's, has always been a mixture of *Realpolitik* and ideology. Because the USSR has been a multinational empire for nearly five centuries, its Great Russian elite has ruled over other nations within the empire. Thus, Russian imperialism abroad was an extension of its internal polity. Tsar Alexander II replied to Western criticism after he had crushed the Polish rising of 1863 that he could not give liberties to his subjects in Poland that he dared not give to his subjects in Russia. The Russian Empire has never had any natural boundaries, only imperial ones.

How different is Soviet foreign policy from Imperial Russia's? Initially, it was less successful because the USSR was weak and isolated. However, Bolshevik ideology gave to Soviet expansionism a conviction of legitimacy and of inevitable success and, paradoxically, the imperative to push history forward faster. The domestic legitimacy and the international communist prestige of the ruling Soviet Communist party have necessarily demanded, and depended on, its claim to represent and lead the irresistible, irreversible course of history toward socialism.

The history of Soviet foreign policy since World War II has been one of a constant, purposeful increase of military power and, under Stalin's successors, of more-flexible, forward strategies to profit from it. Khrushchev began détente with the United States in part to lower the risk of general or nuclear war by accident or miscalculation. Second, he wanted to use it to get U.S. recognition of the status quo in Europe and especially of the division of Germany—Moscow's most valuable gain in World War II. His third aim was the use of détente to lower the risk of Soviet Third World expansion by making forceful U.S. response to it less likely. Successive U.S. administrations explicitly shared his first objective, implicitly shared his second, and until the end of the 1970s, failed to understand his third.

Unlike Stalin, Khrushchev and Brezhnev tried to expand Soviet influence by allying with radical, anticolonial, and anti-U.S. Third World leaders. The results were mixed. In the Middle East, domestic radicalization, sparked by the strains of modernization and intensified by the Arabs' anti-Israeli (and therefore anti-U.S.) impulses, at first helped the Soviets make great progress, notably in Egypt. Moscow faced, however, three obstacles: (1) its failure in Turkey and in Iran, (2) its refusal to fight with the Arabs against Israel lest it risk military confrontation with the United States, and (3) the Arabs' disillusionment with it as a result and the anticommunist revival of fundamentalist Islam.

Once Soviet influence collapsed in Egypt in 1972, its influence in the Middle East and Southwest Asia, many thought, had suffered a major, lasting blow. However, U.S. foreign policy had also been greatly weakened by its defeat in Vietnam and the Watergate scandal. The Vietnam defeat had been in considerable part caused by massive Soviet arms aid to North Vietnam, which the United States, fearing the interruption of détente, had only tried to interrupt at the very end of the war after defeat was inevitable. The United States had long embraced two illusions—namely, that China was Vietnam's principal, most dangerous ally and that it could persuade Moscow to help end the Vietnam War without a U.S. defeat. Behind these errors were two other global ones—the U.S. slowness to understand the Soviet military buildup and the significance of the 1959 Sino-Soviet split.

The USSR considered the United States its strongest and most dangerous short-range enemy and China its most dangerous long-range one. The Soviet military buildup was therefore directed against both. Soviet military deployments against China, the United States, Japan, and Western Europe grew rapidly. Because the Soviets increasingly feared that they would be encircled by a

Sino-U.S.-Japanese-West European alliance, they wanted parity with all their potential enemies and therefore superiority over each one, especially the United States.

Soviet expansion has not operated according to a master plan and timetable. Rather, the Leninist dynamic view of history and duty to push it forward have predisposed Moscow to exploit low-risk opportunities. In the late 1970s, these opportunities were primarily in the Middle East and Southwest Asia. They had arisen in Europe before and might again, and Soviet policy in the Third World, and especially in the Middle East, affects Western Europe as well because of Europe's dependence on oil from the Persian Gulf.

By 1981, the USSR was no longer a model to be imitated in Europe in economics, agriculture, technology, or culture. Only its military power gave it a future to be feared. Since 1948 it had not expanded its influence in Europe. On the contrary, its domination of Yugoslavia and largely of Romania had ended. In the late 1970s, Moscow's gains in Africa, the Middle East, Southwest and Southeast Asia, Angola, Ethiopia, Afghanistan, and Vietnam led to an incipient quadripartite quasi-alliance of the United States, Japan, China, and perhaps eventually Western Europe directed primarily against the USSR.

The USSR also antagonized Japan and drove it closer to the United States and China. It helped to push U.S. policy away from détente toward renewed containment and large-scale rearmament. It made Western Europe more fearful and thereby more difficult to maintain as an "island of détente." By early 1981, its enormously greater military power contrasted sharply with its international near isolation. In theory, it had either to make major concessions to China, to watch it grow more powerful with Western and Japanese aid, or to attack it. The first alternative was unlikely to succeed, and the second and third were equally distasteful to Moscow.

One is struck by the resemblance to 1946-1947. Yet two great differences existed—namely, the United States at that time could have destroyed the USSR with atomic weapons the USSR did not yet possess, and it was not dependent on Middle East oil. By 1981, Moscow and Washington were capable of destroying each other. The USSR had nuclear parity with the United States, conventional superiority, and was building toward naval parity as well. The Third World was more unstable and more actively anti-Western, and the West and Japan were overwhelmingly dependent on Middle East oil.

The United States

In early 1981, the United States was once again changing rapidly—from "malaise," to use President Carter's politically unfortunate term, toward, perhaps, a "great renewal," as President Reagan, politically more profitable, put it. In the late 1970s, a widespread foreboding of decline had spread among the American people, fuelled at home by endemic stagflation, unemployment, the energy crisis, declining industrial productivity, allegedly excessive welfare entitlements, rising Japanese foreign-trade competition, declining industries and real wages, and apparent lack of governmental competence, and abroad by rising Soviet military power and expansionism and by U.S. military failures (for example, Vietnam and the ill-fated Iran rescue attempt) and declining international prestige.[3]

President Carter's 1980 defeat was primarily caused by stagflation and his public image of incompetence. President Reagan's landslide victory may have been a major breakthrough for the U.S. cultural counterrevolution that, to the astonishment of most U.S. intellectuals and almost all Europeans, was by early 1981 under way.

Given the lack in the United States of any decisive alternative, fascist or social-democratic, to liberal-Lockeian capitalism, plus the strong middle- and working-class revulsion, by 1980, against the bohemian ideas and life-styles of radical, secularized intellectuals and media communicators, this cultural counter-revolution predictably proclaimed a virtuous return to older patterns of religion, culture, government, economy, and foreign policy. The counterrevolution was economic, against New Deal welfare capitalism, for the middle and working classes refused to permit so much of their incomes to be redistributed to the under class. In foreign policy it called for the reassertion of U.S. honor and power abroad against the USSR and in the Middle East. The counterrevolution was primarily cultural, however, and in considerable part religious, for above all it proudly proclaimed the return to the good old days and ways; to the un-divorced, patriarchical family; the old-time religion; pre-Keynesian economics; and unalterable hostility to that devilish trinity of abortion, gay liberation, and the Equal Rights Amendment.

The counterrevolution was also regional. It centered in the South, South-west, Midwest, and West—that is, the most rural, suburban, and least "European" parts of the United States. It was strongly individualistic, leaning toward con-servative or libertarian laissez faire. Although it had some parallels in Margaret Thatcher's Britain and in the rising opposition to inflation in continental Europe, it was basically un-European. It was especially so in its religiousness, almost unique to North America, that was little understood and less admired, by most U.S., and by hardly any European, intellectuals. This is not surprising because most leading U.S. intellectuals are as Europeanized and secular as their European counterparts. Why, then, was this counterrevolution so religious?

Most U.S. settlers came from the English and Scotch-Irish nonconformist tradition. They remained the core of U.S. religiosity and its twin, the "civil religion." They hated the English establishment and Anglican and Puritan establishment of the colonies and the early American Republic. They adored Andrew Jackson, the first successful U.S. populist president. As the United States spread westward and developed, its early characteristics—individualism, violence, and ruthless economic competition—intensified. It also was character-ized by an increasingly fragmented ethnic mix and rapid technological change.

The alienation arising from these phenomena fuelled four fundamentalist religious revivals—the four "Great Awakenings." The first of these was in the late colonial period. The others were the anti-Catholic Know-Nothings in the early nineteenth century, the evangelism of Dwight C. Moody and Billy Sunday in the early twentieth century that brought prohibition, and by 1981, the fourth had as its core the Moral Majority.

All of these Great Awakenings were antiestablishment, antisecularist, populist, and middle- and lower-class based. All, like Thoreau, "turned toward Oregon"—away from the immorality, corruption, greed, and wars of Europe and of the Europeanized East Coast establishment. All were morally and politically rigid, Puritanical, and antiintellectual.

Secularization, however, not the Awakenings, has usually won the day. Many leading creative U.S. intellectuals in the twentieth century either emigrated to Europe, like Pound, Eliot, Stein, or Hemingway, or became "internal émigrés" like Faulkner, Mencken, or Twain. It is therefore doubtful that the Fourth Awakening can indefinitely reverse the secularization of modern developed societies. Yet recent history, notably in the Middle East, makes one wonder if any developed society can remain indefinitely stable without some kind of religion, other worldly or ersatz. We shall see.

The U.S. cultural counterrevolution we are discussing has been, uniquely, ideologically led by a small group of first-rate intellectuals, the so-called neo-conservatives, most of whom were irreligious, Jewish, and former radical leftists.[4] They preached conservative values, notably the family. They rejected the "Viet-nam syndrome," "McGovernism"—that is, the revolution of entitlements, the nonuse of force abroad, priority for the Third World, and "anti-anticommunism." Jewish neoconservatives were also influenced by their hostility to reverse dis-crimination (beginning with the Ocean Hill–Brownsville case), their fervent support for Israel, and their hostility to Soviet antisemitism.

However, some of the neoconservative intellectuals were not Jewish. More important, mass support for conservatism was Protestant and Catholic. Its roots were in populism, Protestant (and Catholic) fundamentalism, and revolt against inflation. One should not overestimate its significance. But what *was* new in the United States in mid-1981, what did not exist to the same extent or form in Western Europe, and what was strongly anti-USSR in theory and practice was the symbiosis of neoconservative intellectuals and an organized, politically activist conservative mass movement.

The current Fourth Awakening was primarily important for U.S. foreign policy because, like the Third, it was strongly anti-USSR. But unlike the East Coast Establishment, also traditionally anti-Soviet but favorably inclined toward Western Europe, it was culturally and religiously nationalist, opposed to the Protestant social gospel that tried to help the poor at home and Third World–liberation movements abroad, and doubtful about why the United States must spend so much for Western Europe's defense while the West Europeans spent so little to defend themselves. In sum, the new U.S. conservatives were hostile to the USSR, critical of Western Europe, and little concerned about the Third World.

The change in public opinion in the United States in the late 1970s was drastic and rapid indeed.[5] In 1976, in the aftermath of Vietnam and Watergate, the United States was badly split, flailing about in a wave of self-examination and self-doubt, determined to restore honesty to the White House, and strongly for détente. Only four years later, after the shocks of Iran and Afghanistan, the Soviet military buildup, and Cuban involvement overseas, a major change occurred in public opinion, one of those that sometimes result in critical political realignments. By 1981, most Americans wanted to recover control of the economy and foreign affairs and to regain their honor and reassert their power by, for example, greater toughness abroad, higher military spending, less priority for human rights and more for CIA operations, and the use of trade and aid for foreign policy purposes. They were much more concerned with the Soviet threat and much less with the Third World. They even wanted, by a small but significant majority, the reinstitution of compulsory military service, which seemed incredible only five years after the fall of Saigon.

This change was not surprising because few nations, and certainly not the United States, easily digest defeat or long engage in self-criticism. The change, which had begun about 1975,[6] accelerated rapidly in the late 1970s and interacted with the revival of religious fundamentalism. By then most Americans believed that not only the economy and foreign affairs but also that crime, sex, and morality were out of control. By 1981 the Moral Majority, and many other people, believed that the United States must return to religion, frugality, morality, the work ethic, and honor and power in foreign affairs. Such is a consummation perhaps devoutly to be wished but still difficult to combine, one might think, with the sophistication, compromise, and knowledge required of U.S. foreign policy in, for example, the Middle East or to win approval from skeptical, cynical, world-weary Western Europeans, most of whom viewed this trend with alarm (insofar as they understood it), as another example of U.S. naiveté, fickleness, and threat to détente.

The Global Perspective

In early 1981, seven principal developments dominated international politics.[7] The first was the continuing Soviet military buildup toward global power and influence at least equal to that of all its potential enemies. Two motives for this buildup reinforced each other. The first was expansionist—that is, Moscow's lunge for global power. The other was defensive—that is, its preemptive breakout into the "arc of crisis" in the Middle East and Southwest and Southeast Asia, where oil dependence, the Palestinian issue, and Islamic fundamentalism weakened the West, in order to foil looming Soviet encirclement by China, the United States, Japan, and West Germany.[8] This move instead created, as Imperial Germany had, the encirclement it feared: the Chinese-initiated attempt, with the United States by 1981 a reluctant, limited partner, to encircle the USSR— a quasi-alliance with the beginnings of a military dimension between Washington and Beijing. Second, after surmounting the Vietnam syndrome, the United States began to strengthen its military power and to revive its will to use it. Third, the unsuccessful 1979 attack on the Grand Mosque in Mecca and the 1980 Iraqi-Iranian War and the threat of its spreading underlined the instability of the Middle East, an essential source of energy for the United States, Western Europe, and Japan, but an area where in 1981 the USSR was superior in ground-based air power to the West and Japan. Indeed, increasing instability in the Third World created opportunities that neither the USSR nor the United States was willing not to exploit. Fifth, conservatism was rising in the United States and the USSR. The sixth development, the decline in U.S. support for priority in arms-control negotiations, had major implications for U.S. relations with Western Europe as well as with the USSR. Seventh, all these developments so intensified Soviet-U.S. competition that Soviet-U.S. détente gave way to a second cold war in the underdeveloped world, with only Western Europe remaining an island of détente.[9]

Moscow believed that because of its geographical position and the nuclear forces arrayed against it, actually or potentially, by all other major nuclear powers, the USSR should have nuclear parity with them all. Washington rejected the nuclear inferiority that Moscow's aim required. In the European theater, the USSR was deploying SS-20s, and NATO had decided to deploy in reply modernized long-range-theater nuclear forces [LRTNF, including Pershing II-As and ground-launched cruise missiles (GLCMs)] targeted from West European launching sites on the USSR. Some two-thirds of Soviet SS-20s were targeted on Western Europe, around one-third were targeted on China, and around one-half of them all were retargetable from Western Europe to China and vice versa. Thus, the USSR had to reject a distinction between intercontinental and Euro-strategic nuclear weapons for it felt it necessary to have as many missiles targeted on the United States, Western Europe, and China together as all three had targeted against it.

Of these developments, the three that had the most effect on Soviet-U.S. relations and on Europe were the Soviet military buildup, the U.S. disillusionment with arms-control negotiations, and the instability of the Middle East and Southwest Asia. The first two were closely interrelated. They led to increasing differences of view between not only the United States and the USSR but also between the United States and West Germany, Belgium, and the Netherlands. (France had never participated in arms-control negotiations, and Great Britain was so dependent on U.S. help to maintain its own independent nuclear deterrent that it never seriously differed with U.S. policy.)

That the USSR has over the last two decades carried out a massive nuclear, conventional, and naval buildup could by 1981 no longer be disputed, for in the SALT I and II negotiations, the USSR had accepted U.S. statistics on its nuclear forces as a basis for negotiations and U.S. satellite photography made concealment difficult, if not impossible.

By early 1981, the USSR had exceeded the United States in nuclear throw weight; it was approaching parity in nuclear warheads; it was rapidly modernizing its Eurostrategic nuclear forces; it was building a seven-ocean blue-water navy; it had increased its tank and air capabilities on the European central front; it had simultaneously built up a major, nuclear-armed, more-than-forty-division force on the Chinese border; and it had deployed military advisors and the troops of its Cuban ally in Angola and Ethiopia and some 85,000 Red Army troops in Afghanistan.

Moscow maintained that all this was not contrary to but rather furthered détente. As Brezhnev said in 1969 (before Angola, Ethiopia, and Afghanistan), "Peaceful coexistence . . . creates the most favorable conditions for the construction of a new society in the socialist countries, for the development of the revolutionary and liberating movement."[10] He also declared that:

> [E]ven under . . . conditions of sharp political and ideological struggle between socialism and capitalism in the international arena, practical steps in the direction of disarmament can and should be taken.[11]

To translate this into U.S. jargon, Brezhnev was opposed to "linkage." (So, until the Soviet invasion of Afghanistan, was President Carter). President Reagan, however, declared in early 1981 that he favored it.

For Moscow détente combined, first, superpower crisis management to lower the risk of nuclear war by accident or miscalculation, to further crisis management for that purpose, and to codify nuclear parity with the United States with, second, and with less risk to itself, intensified Soviet competition with the United States in the Third World, primarily by arms aid and transport and supply of Cuban troops, in order to expand both the world revolution and Soviet influence. Thus, that any American ever thought Moscow would think or act differently was the result of his own naiveté, not Moscow's concealment of its views.

Soviet views on arms control, unsurprisingly, have not been uniform. Some Soviet military theorists gave it low priority and stressed the importance of nuclear-war-fighting capability and Soviet nuclear superiority. Some Soviet civilian theorists stressed the destructiveness of nuclear war and advocated arms-control agreements on the basis of strategic parity with the United States. All of them, however, rejected linkage, advocated Soviet support of "national liberation movements,"[12] and emphasized that arms-control agreements had only become possible because the correlation of forces (that is, of military power) had shifted in Soviet favor. To prevent guerrilla wars (and Soviet military aid to them) has thus, unlike the United States, never been a Soviet purpose. Rather Moscow has used arms control to make these wars less risky and therefore more profitable to the USSR.[13] This has included a Soviet nuclear- and conventional-war-fighting capability to try to deny escalation dominance to the United States.

The USSR has always believed that history is dynamic, not stable, and that it is inevitably moving toward the so-called worldwide victory of socialism. Moreover, as is usual with imperial powers, although the USSR often acted defensively, from its own viewpoint, the results thereof soon became transformed into expansionist gains and whetted Soviet appetites for more.

The Sino-Soviet split made Moscow compete with Beijing, especially in Asia, more than it would have against the United States alone. Thus Moscow's often subjectively defensive moves seemed expansionist to Washington and Beijing, while Moscow increasingly suspected them of uniting to encircle it— another self-fulfilling prophecy.

The U.S. Malaise about Détente

The minimal U.S. détente objectives have been limitation of the risk of nuclear war, an objective the USSR has shared, and limitation of defense expenditures and adjustment to limitation of U.S. foreign commitments after the Vietnam War and Watergate, from both of which the USSR intended to, and did, profit. Whenever the USSR has proposed détente, the West has usually not long been able to or willing to resist agreeing to it. This was true for the United States after Vietnam and Watergate, and since 1945 it has been true for Western Europe, in part because of its weakness vis-à-vis rising Soviet military power.

That a malaise about détente had developed in the United States during the previous five years was quite clear by 1981. It covered all aspects of East-West détente, most of all the military one. By 1981 this malaise had become so much stronger in the United States than in Western Europe that U.S.-West European relations worsened as a result.

Most Americans felt that Soviet actions were the principal cause of the Western malaise with détente. In my view, however, as important a cause was the initially exaggerated U.S. expectations about détente—that it would lead to international stability. These expectations were baseless. Not only had the Soviets never said or done anything to justify them but they had said and done exactly the opposite. There were also historical and psychological causes of the U.S. malaise about détente. Most Americans are optimistic by heritage, and many West Europeans would like to be optimistic so as not to have to face up to their own weakness. Their leaders reflected and indeed often further exaggerated these hopes, for being for peace is usually electorally profitable. Chamberlain's optimism about Hitler and Roosevelt's about Stalin were neither

the first nor the last illusory and self-serving but baseless and misleading optimistic pronouncements by democratic statesmen about their enemies.

Another major cause of the U.S. malaise about détente was the resentment
of Soviet and East European repression of dissidents. Détente favored dissidence
in the East more than in the West. Both East and West wanted to bring radical
dissidence under control. However, Eastern repression was much greater and
usually more newsworthy than Western at a time when U.S. optimists believed,
or at least hoped, that détente would make the East less repressive. What an
illusion—if the East were successfully to contain détente's destabilization, its
repression *had* to increase.

One aspect of Soviet repression—Moscow's harassment of pro-Zionist Soviet
Jews and its refusal to let some of them emigrate—was a reaction to the revival
of Zionism among Soviet Jewry subsequent to the 1967 Middle East War. In the
United States it became one of the major causes of the rising malaise with
détente, primarily because the U.S. Jewish community is far larger and more
influential than in the West European countries and also more tied to Israel,
whose government decided to make a major issue of the matter.

The United States was not the only Western country in which special factors affected public sentiment about détente. West Germany was another. In no
other West European country was sentiment for détente so strong because most
West Germans came to feel that by increasing or at least maintaining human ties
with East Germany, détente furthered German national as well as humanitarian aims.

Another development, particularly in France, Italy, and Spain, also deepened
the Western malaise about détente—that is, the collapse of the attractiveness of
the Soviet model of ideology, economy, technology, politics, culture, and
society. This development was difficult to quantify but unmistakable in the
intellectual communities of Paris and Rome and New York as well. Soviet repression and technological backwardness were its two main causes. Moscow's
military power was more feared, but its society was no longer something worthy
of emulation. This development also played a role in the rise of Eurocommunism,
the opposition of which to Soviet political and ideological hegemony further
discredited and delegitimatized Soviet real socialism.

Détente was stabilizing *and* destabilizing, particularly in Europe. Détente
made it harder for Moscow to keep up East-West communication barriers in
Europe because the West made progress toward their dismantlement a precondition to agreement to Soviet détente initiatives. Détente therefore increased
cultural and economic interpenetration between West and East in Europe.

The USSR insisted upon the "intensification of the ideological struggle"
during détente for two reasons. The first reason was offensive: Moscow believed
that détente made forward policies in the Third World less risky. The second
was defensive: Western ideological, economic, and technological penetration
into Eastern Europe encouraged dissidence there, while Soviet propaganda in

the West was usually unsuccessful, except about the Vietnam War and the neutron bomb. The USSR and its East European allies therefore intensified their repression of dissidence, which in turn partially restabilized Eastern Europe but strengthened opposition to détente in the West.

Détente at first lowered the West's perception of the Soviet threat. It therefore made it more difficult to maintain, and even more so to increase, Western defense expenditures in order to match the Soviet military buildup. The USSR expected to get political payoffs from its rising military power by influencing West European states to be more amenable to Moscow's wishes. However, the Soviet military buildup produced a counterreaction—that is, the West began to increase defense budgets. This escalating military competition eroded détente.

Détente normally limits, but during regional crises it can also increase, regional superpower tension. Global superpower détente aids superpower crisis management and thus in theory lowers the risk that escalating regional crises will lead to general or nuclear war. However, in the 1973 Middle East War, superpower brinkmanship may have been greater because, given global détente and nuclear near parity, both superpowers thought it was less dangerous.

The decline of the Western perception of the Soviet threat made it easier for the "alienation of affluence," often characteristic of rebellious Western youths, to become politically destabilizing (for example, in France in May 1968 and later in Italy). It also helped increase the strength in Western Europe of the Left, including the Communist parties. However, détente also favored dissidence in Eastern Europe. In West Germany it helped to integrate rebellious youths. Finally, in Portugal it made Soviet political intervention counterproductive. In sum, as Pierre Hassner perceptively put it:

> In this new phase [détente] characterized by ambiguity and contradiction, the isolation can be broken, but in favor of a penetration which is asymmetrical and not equilibrated rather than by reconciliation. There can always be enough fermentation to prevent stability by freezing, enough separation and divergence to stop stability by integration. The essential characteristic of "hot peace" is neither force nor cooperation but the constant reciprocal influence of societies within a competition whose aims are less and less tangible, whose means are less and less direct, whose consequences are less and less calculable, precisely because these activities will be as important for their effects on what societies *are* as on what they *do*. . . .

> What characterizes all negotiations in the age of hot peace is the importance of the time dimension and therefore of uncertainty and betting: rarely has diplomacy (as also the use of force) so been based on implicit bets about its effect on long-term processes . . . about which no one can know to what point troops and treaties can manipulate, reverse, influence, control or limit them. . . .

> Hot peace does not necessarily break the equilibrium between alliances and societies, but it tends to make each more vulnerable to the other.

From the moment when the existence and legitimacy of the structure are confirmed, the real competition, intentional or involuntary, begins. . . .[14]

Increased ideological interpenetration was more destabilizing in the East than in the West. The alienation of affluence had little mass base in Western Europe and by 1981 less in the United States. The causes of political destabilization in Western Europe have been increased energy costs, trade union pressures, governmental corruption, terrorism, and so on, not ideological infection from the socialist East.

Finally, there was another, reverse asymmetry. The USSR has been ready, willing, and able, as it showed in Budapest in 1956 and Prague in 1968, to intervene militarily to counteract major destabilization in Eastern Europe, while one could imagine only with great difficulty that the United States would intervene militarily for the same stabilizing reason in Western Europe. Finally, Moscow's intervention in Angola, Ethiopia, and Afghanistan gravely eroded détente.

The Sino-Soviet Factor

The Sino-Soviet split helped intensify East-West détente in the early 1970s. Khrushchev's initiation of détente with the West after Stalin's death was not primarily caused by concern about Sino-Soviet relations. However, this probably played a role, albeit a secondary one, in the new Soviet leadership's decision to initiate détente with the West. Khrushchev's foreign policy in 1953–1955 also included a more-forward foreign policy toward the Third World, one then directed much more against the West than China. However, his first foreign trip was to China in 1954, and in 1955 in Moscow he urged Adenauer to help him in his relations with China.[15]

Sino-Soviet relations were first seriously strained in 1957 and collapsed in 1959.[16] Thereafter the Soviets began a political offensive and a military buildup against China. Both of these intensified after the failure of the Soviet attempt, after Khrushchev's removal in late 1964, at a partial rapprochement with Beijing. Sino-Soviet hostility culminated in the 1969 border incidents on the Ussuri and in Xinjiang. Although Moscow thereafter compelled Beijing to cease the border clashes, tension remained high. Even before that, the 1968 Soviet invasion of Czechoslovakia was probably the immediate cause for the Chinese decision to improve relations with the United States. Conversely, after the first Ussuri border incident, the Soviets suddenly ceased harassment of West Berlin, one of the first signs of their desire to stabilize their European flank. In 1971, Kissinger successfully put pressure on Moscow to move toward détente by showing that the United States had another alternative—namely, alliance with Beijing against the USSR. Thus, in the 1960s and 1970s, the Chinese leaders who wanted partial détente with Moscow were always defeated.[17] The Sino-Soviet split thus initially intensified détente in Europe because Moscow wanted to keep its Western flank quiet when it was so preoccupied with a hostile China and because Washington successfully used its Chinese connection to intensify détente. However, because the Sino-Soviet split intensified the Soviet military buildup, it later helped intensify the U.S. malaise about détente with the USSR.

After Mao died in 1976, the Soviets tried hard to achieve a partial détente in Sino-Soviet state relations, but they refused to make major concessions to Beijing on either the unequal-treaties issue, the disputed territories (several hundred islands in the Amur and Ussuri Rivers), or on their de facto claim to primacy among Communist parties. The Chinese rejected the Soviet overtures, Sino-Soviet border negotiations again were broken off, and Moscow resumed polemics with Beijing, which it had suspended when Mao died. Beijing sharpened its verbal attacks on Moscow and tried to set up an anti-Soviet alliance of the United States, Western Europe, Japan, and the Third World. There were several indications of how far the new Chinese leadership was prepared to go in this direction—for example, Tito's triumphal 1977 visit to Beijing (despite the fact that Beijing still officially considered him a revisionist); a Chinese statement that while it considered the West European Communist parties to be revisionist, it supported their opposition to Soviet hegemony; Hua's return visit to Bucharest and Belgrade in 1978; the resumption of Sino-Yugoslav party relations; and finally, the resumption of party relations betwen the Chinese and the Italian party in 1979 and the Spanish in 1980. On the latter occasion, the Chinese said that they considered all parties absolutely equal, made no claim to communist hegemony, and did not hold the doctrine of the inevitability of war—that is, did not object to the West European parties' support of détente. Beijing was much more actively involved against Moscow in the European Communist parties than it had been during its abortive attempt in the 1960s to set up Maoist parties there. Although Albania broke with China, the Sino-Yugoslav rapprochement more than compensated for it.

By 1981, several other developments had again worsened Sino-Soviet relations. The most important was hostilities in Indochina—namely, the Soviet-supported Vietnamese invasion and near conquest of Chinese-supported Cambodia and as a result, the brief, limited Chinese invasion of the extreme northern part of Vietnam. Their causes were primarily regional because of the age-old Vietnamese determination to dominate Indochina and China's historic determination to do the same. Sino-Vietnamese hostilities broke out because the near century of French and then U.S. influence in Vietnam had been replaced by Soviet influence, and Moscow was trying to encircle China just as China was trying to encircle it. China continued to support the Pol Pot guerrillas in Cambodia, while the USSR got the use of the (ex-U.S.) naval and air bases at Da Nang and Cam Ranh Bay. Even if the other Sino-Soviet issues could be compromised, which in 1981 seemed most unlikely, their conflicting interests and policies in Indochina made any overall compromise the more unlikely. The reason for this was that Moscow thought that China was trying to encircle the USSR—as indeed it was—by a Sino-Japanese-West European-U.S. alliance against it, while Beijing thought that the USSR was trying to encircle China—as indeed it also was—through its alliance with Vietnam. Moreover, Hanoi's motives were not identical with Moscow's: Hanoi feared traditional Chinese hegemony over Indochina, was determined to dominate Indochina itself, and only the USSR was available to help it in these objectives. Conversely, because Hanoi was not controlled by Moscow but only allied with it, and because, through hostile acts toward Beijing undertaken at its own initiative, Hanoi could make a Sino-Soviet rapprochement much more difficult, Hanoi thus became an autonomous factor in Sino-Soviet relations, likely to disrupt any rapprochement between the two.

After 1971, Soviet-U.S. détente was partly based on, and furthered by, Moscow's and Beijing's desire to improve relations with Washington lest it ally with one against the other. This U.S. "China card" limited Moscow's and Beijing's, and increased Washington's, freedom of maneuver. Moscow therefore sought a partial (state-level) détente with Beijing, inter alia to devalue this card. Such a Sino-Soviet détente, in the prevailing view in Washington, would be contrary to U.S. interests because in a period of rising Soviet and relatively declining U.S. military power, Sino-Soviet hostility helped insure rough Soviet-U.S. parity.

After normalization with the United States and limited war with Hanoi, Beijing proposed in early 1979 to negotiate with Moscow for the first time without preconditions. The first round of negotiations ended on 30 November 1979 without any agreement. The Soviets proposed a declaration to endorse equality, independence, sovereignty, territorial integrity, and nonthreat of force. The Chinese insisted upon specific agreements about withdrawal of Soviet support from Vietnam and of Soviet troops along the Sino-Soviet and Sino-Mongolian borders and about the disputed territories. The negotiations were scheduled to resume in Beijing, but the Chinese canceled them after the Soviet invasion of Afghanistan. By 1981, Sino-Soviet relations were worse than at any time since 1969.

Defense, Détente, and Arms Control

You Americans will never be able to do this to us again.—Kuznetsov to McCloy (1963)[18]

There is no indication that the Soviets are seeking to develop a strategic nuclear force as large as ours.—Robert McNamara (1964)[19]

Arms control has essentially failed.—Leslie H. Gelb (1979)[20]

U.S. elite and mass opinion had by 1981 turned away from arms-control agreements with the USSR in favor of defense buildup and linkage.[21] This occurred more in elite than mass opinion for, while a majority still supported SALT in principle, elite pessimism was shown by the contrast between the optimism of the path-breaking 1960 *Daedalus* special number on arms control and the pessimism prevalent in its two special numbers on defense in 1980-1981. Compare also the near-unanimous Senate ratification of SALT I with the major resistance to SALT II and its blocking by the "Soviet Brigade in Cuba" episode and the Soviet invasion of Afghanistan.

In the United States, arms control claimed the status of an academic discipline and arms controllers became a civilian guild with, at least until recently, a strong commitment to the primacy of arms control in U.S. foreign policy. Conversely, many U.S.-defense specialists and the great majority of the U.S. military, although usually not opposed to arms control per se, gave priority to their vow of national security, whether by increasing defense budgets, bringing about arms-control agreements with fewer concessions to the Soviets, or both.

In the USSR, the situation was quite different. Although a few high civilian officials in the central committee secretariat, the foreign ministry, and the various research institutes concerned themselves with arms control inter alia, most Soviet officials who dealt with it were military officers. (Remember the episode in the SALT I negotiations when the senior Soviet military representative indicated his concern about U.S. negotiators' discussing Soviet nuclear capability with the Soviet civilian negotiators.) For Moscow, arms control was one part of a grand strategy, the context of which contributed to lowering the risk of nuclear war; to demobilizing the United States and its allies so that they would be less likely to reply to Soviet military buildup and arms aid to Third World national liberation movements; and to limiting extensive U.S. deployment of new military technology.

Why did SALT gain such support in the United States in the 1970s but lose so much of it by the 1980s? After World War II, arms control became an article of faith for U.S. liberals because of their fear of a nuclear catastrophe; their consequent belief that the avoidance of such a catastrophe must be given absolute priority; and their conviction that the nuclear danger could indeed be reduced and that Moscow and Washington should have such a common commitment to this start that it would override their competitiveness on the arms-control issue. Indeed, in the 1960s many U.S. arms controllers, including Secretary of Defense Robert McNamara, thought that the United States should teach the USSR about arms control—for example, that the USSR had no real reason to build up to nuclear parity with the United States. One's mind boggles, in retrospect, at this combination of historical naiveté and unconscious chauvinism. Soviet minds must have boggled as well for they did just the opposite. U.S. participants in the détente-sparked Soviet-U.S. discussion groups on arms control frequently held these same school-masterish views. However, while the U.S. academic and governmental arms-control community often influenced U.S. policies, they, like other Americans, had few contacts with Soviet central committee or military personnel who determined the Soviet position.

U.S. support for arms control was much strengthened by the Vietnam experience that, many arms controllers believed, further demonstrated the danger of massive use of military force and by the rush forward in military technology, the prohibition or limitation of which became a part of arms-control doctrine. By the early 1970s, U.S. strategic doctrine accepted, and indeed some officials even favored, nuclear parity with the USSR—something to which the USSR, given its numerical inferiority and its massive nuclear buildup, had every reason to agree.

Some U.S. arms controllers doubted if even parity was necessary. Would not the so-called assured destruction capability be enough? Nixon and Kissinger spoke of entangling the USSR in so many cooperative relationships that a stable structure of peace would finally emerge. (Kissinger, a historical pessimist, hoped that this would restrain the Soviet thrust for global power.) The majority of the U.S. arms-control community long supported the doctrine of nuclear stability through "mutual assured destruction" (MAD)—that is, that because there is no way of becoming invulnerable to destruction, each side should have an invulnerable second-strike-deterrent force targeted on urban and industrial areas (countervalue strategy), for little if anything more than that would be needed. Historical optimists, they thought that the USSR would also accept MAD. U.S. conservatives combined pessimism about the USSR with optimism about the United States being able, and capable of being brought to be willing, to maintain or recover numerical superiority or at least parity. Furthermore, in the early 1970s Moscow (as well as Washington) opposed antiballistic-missile (ABM) deployment because U.S. ABM technology was then far ahead of the Soviet technology.

In the 1960s and early 1970s, U.S. public opinion was pro–arms control. Moreover, there were then no major verification and fewer blurring problems (between strategic, Eurostrategic, or conventional weapons). However, even then, a minority, largely civilians, opposed MAD and, beginning in 1959, stressed that U.S. nuclear targeting (under the single integrated operational plan, or SIOP) should be not only countervalue but should also include more economic, political, and Soviet nuclear and other force targets (some of which had always been targeted), with options as to which sets of targets might be attacked.

Why did the tide turn? Some reasons for this have already been discussed: the rise of conservatism, the Soviet military buildup, and the rapid decline of the Vietnam syndrome.[22] Soviet gains in Angola, Ethiopia, Vietnam, and especially Afghanistan were also important causes. The closer the USSR came to nuclear parity, the more U.S. conservatives suspected that Moscow was reaching for perceived nuclear superiority. Indeed, by 1981 many conservatives believed that the USSR already had it or would soon get it, and some wanted the United States to reacquire it. Soviet Eurostrategic modernization and naval buildup strengthened this feeling. When the Red Army invaded Afghanistan in December 1979, most Americans (although fewer Europeans) believed that Moscow had, for the first time since World War II, by invading a country not in the Warsaw Pact, broken the rules of the game, and must be contained for the invasion brought the Red Army and Air Force to within 500 miles of the Strait of Hormuz, reinforced the impact of the collapse of U.S. influence in Iran, and highlighted Soviet military strength, in contrast to U.S. weakness, with respect to the oil supplies, indispensible for the West and Japan, from the Persian Gulf.

The New Military Technology

In early 1981 the new post–SALT I weapons systems deployed or under development had originated almost entirely in the United States[23]. (The USSR was at least several years behind.) The overall impact of these systems on arms control seemed likely to be negative. (In theory, however, cruise missiles could provide an invulnerable second-strike capability and therefore stability.) They made an agreed definition of nuclear and conventional parity more difficult. They posed new, serious obstacles to verification. They so further blurred the distinction between nuclear and conventional weapons that they logically outmoded the existing arms-control-negotiation frameworks. They strengthened the Soviet fear that the United States alone—leaving aside the nuclear forces of France, Great Britain, West Germany, China, and Japan—was trying for, and might well recover, at least the appearance of nuclear superiority over the USSR.

These new weapons systems resulted from breakthroughs in information collection, concealment, processing, and distribution. They were the products of several new advanced technologies: much more-accurate guidance systems; much smaller and more-effective jet engines; more-miniaturized nuclear and conventional warheads; more-advanced electronic intelligence (ELINT) and electronic countermeasures (ECM); improved command, control, communication, and intelligence systems (C^3I); low-altitude flight and low radar reflectability, which degrade hostile air defenses; small remotely piloted vehicles (RPVs) for television target acquisition and designation; and the new technologies of sensors and large-scale integration (LSI) of electronic circuits.

They may be divided into three families: (1) MIRV and MaRV—multiple independently targetable reentry and maneuverable reentry vehicles on strategic missiles, whose high-precision guidance and consequent terminal accuracy were based on complex microelectronic information-processing and retargeting systems; (2) cruise missiles (CMs)—air-, sea-, and land-launched, precision-guided airborne drones with nuclear or conventional warheads, made possible by much smaller and more-efficient jet engines and miniaturization of conventional and nuclear warheads, whose trajectory was adjustable in flight by a terrain-matching (TERCOM) or (in the future) satellite guidance system, with circular error of probability (CEP) accuracy of about 100 meters and ranges up to 2,000 miles; and (3) air- and ground-launched precision-guided conventional munitions (PGMs)—extremely accurate antiaircraft and antitank weapons with a CEP of 10 meters, which greatly increased tank and airplane vulnerability, as the Egyptian use of Soviet PGMs in the 1973 Middle East War demonstrated.

The key technological breakthroughs were relatively unrelated—that is, they were not the result of one overall research program. These breakthroughs profited from the advances in miniaturization and reliability that the U.S. space program produced, from the OECD-wide R&D base of the largely U.S.-owned multinational corporations, and from the encouragement in the United States (as opposed to the de facto discouragement in the USSR) of spin-off from military to civilian industrial sectors and vice versa.

All these systems were much more difficult to verify. They combined higher accuracy; longer range; smaller size; greater but more discriminating destructiveness; easier transportability, launching, and concealment; and a much higher cost-benefit ratio—the fulfillment of "Engine Charlie" Wilson's dream in the Eisenhower era of "a bigger bang for a buck."

Before the election of President Reagan, U.S. CM deployment seemed to some people to be endangered by two factors: (1) the precedent, if continued, of the SALT II protocol's limitation on range because of Soviet pressure and (2) the bureaucratic threat to U.S. manned bombers and large attack carriers. (Historically, bureaucratic resistance to new weapons has caused long delays in their deployment.) However, the protocol would soon expire, and in early 1981 it seemed that the Reagan administration, committed to a higher defense budget, might speed up CM development and deployment. Nevertheless, CM technological problems and low cost-effectiveness remained obstacles to rapid deployment.

The implications for détente and the military balance in Europe of CM and PGM deployment were considerable. Long-range air- or sea-launched CMs blurred the distinction between strategic and conventional arms and therefore between SALT and Mutual (and Balanced) Force Reduction [M(B)FR]. The difficulty of their verifiability and the fact that they could operate from launching sites outside regional areas such as Central Europe made M(B)FR more difficult.

CMs also raised problems for Soviet and U.S. relations with Western Europe, particularly with West Germany. They had such increased range and accuracy for delivery of conventional explosives, through technologies the West Europeans could acquire, that they could enable the West Europeans to compensate considerably and rapidly for the Soviet military buildup on the Central European front, particularly if the United States would transfer CM technology to the West Europeans. Moscow maintained that the SALT II protocol prohibited this, and although Washington declared that it did not, the issue caused concern in Western Europe.

New U.S. weapons technologies, however, could not soon outstrip the Soviet military buildup. The situation in early 1981 seemed to be that the United States was ahead in R&D and the USSR in deployment.

The USSR made some, but not as much, progress as the United States in PGMs. Although in 1981 they had not yet developed equivalent CMs, their past record indicated that they would. However, by then the United States would probably have made further technological advances, especially in C^3I. The Soviets had been trying to overcome the U.S. qualitative lead by further increasing weapons production and deployment, notably in missile throw weight and tanks, in which they were already superior, as well as by arms-control negotiations.

Weapons technology was thus developing rapidly, with significant political implications for Soviet-U.S. relations and for the relations of both superpowers with Europe. While the U.S. technological R&D lead was likely to be maintained, it would hardly be sufficient to swamp the USSR, which would continue to have the capability, and certainly the will, to catch up. Moreover, PGMs and CMs, for example, were not very effective in bad weather and would need some time to get all the bugs out of them. These new weapons systems, because of their complexity and cost, were likely to be largely limited to the superpowers and would further increase the military technological gap between them and the West European powers, who would therefore become dependent on the United States for assistance in maintaining the credibility of their own nuclear forces and providing the essential overarching nuclear deterrent for Western Europe.

In addition to MaRV, which could limit the cost-effectiveness of any ballistic missile defense (BMD) deployment, CMs and PGMs were available. In 1981 other, even newer U.S. weapons systems were in R&D. They included advanced strategic air-launched cruise missiles (ASALM), strategic bombers and advanced maneuvering and precision-guided reentry vehicles (AMaRV and PGRV), new BMD technology, and perhaps directed-energy weapons (DEW) such as high-energy lasers. Most of them featured greater accuracy and penetrability, including against C^3I. While no decisive anti-submarine warfare (ASW) developments seemed likely in the near future, these additional new developments, and those already in deployment, would further destabilize the superpower military rivalry for several reasons. For instance, they could increase the temptation for a nuclear first strike. They tended to lower predictability because they made surveillance, intelligence collection, and therefore verifiability more difficult. They blurred further the usual distinctions among weapons systems and arms-control negotiations. Finally, they further outmoded MAD strategy and made a nuclear-war-fighting strategy technologically more possible.

It may turn out that the 1960s and early 1970s were an exception, not the rule, a period during which superpower arms-control agreements were both possible and desirable for in those years there was both a political motive, détente, and a technologically favorable environment—large, invulnerable, verifiable, unblurred intercontinental ballistic missiles (ICBMs). By 1981, the latter's invulnerability was going fast, and détente was in great peril. No wonder that arms controllers were pessimistic and many strategists had written off arms control.

Nuclear Nonproliferation

The United States has been in a dilemma in respect to nuclear proliferation since the rapid Soviet thermonuclear buildup. Should it maintain the Soviet-U.S. nuclear duopoly even if that would mean accepting Soviet nuclear parity or even superiority, or should it tolerate or even encourage its allies' gaining or increasing their nuclear capabilities in order to compensate for the Soviet nuclear buildup? The conscious U.S. reason for not doing the latter has been its desire to restrain nuclear proliferation as much as possible on the theory that because more nuclear powers mean more chances of nuclear war, Soviet-U.S. nuclear duopoly helps nuclear stability. Other, sometimes unconscious, U.S. motives have been the fear that nuclear proliferation would weaken the U.S. position vis-à-vis its (nuclear) allies and thus make nuclear stability more difficult to achieve and manage; the great-power chauvinism historically characteristic of major powers; the force of habit; and finally, the firm, sometimes almost theological, belief that nuclear weapons are so destructive that they are bad by definition and therefore their proliferation must be restrained—particularly to those nonnuclear powers ("lesser breeds without the law"?) who neither understand how to or, perhaps, wish to put the nuclear djin back into its bottle.

There has never been a decisive movement in Washington against nonproliferation since the late 1950s when Eisenhower stationed tactical nuclear weapons in Europe under the one- or two-key systems. The ill-fated multilateral nuclear force (MLF) was intended in part to further nonproliferation (by guarding against Bonn's demanding national nuclear weapons). Its sinking by Lyndon Johnson confirmed the U.S. trend toward nonproliferation, nuclear duopoly, and bilateral Soviet-U.S. SALT negotiations in preference to maximizing alliance strength. Conversely, more-complex ICBM technology and Soviet and U.S. advantages in it discouraged the British and French from acquiring more than minimal nuclear forces. President Carter's more-active nonproliferation policy initially worsened U.S. relations with Western Europe, but later some common interests developed, even with France—for example, to prevent proliferation in South Asia.

Soviet-U.S. Nuclear Doctrinal Asymmetry

There had always been a major asymmetry between many U.S. and all Soviet published strategic nuclear analyses.[24] Many U.S. arms-control theorists (but never the U.S. government) supported MAD. Extreme MAD doctrine required avoidance of positive defense because, it argued, it would be ineffective and there was no alternative to acceptance of, indeed even desire for, invulnerable countervalue second-strike-deterrence capability by one's opponent as well as oneself.

Soviet strategic thinkers, however, while recognizing that mutual deterrence existed and was minimally desirable, also insisted that nuclear defense, by avoiding defeat, made nuclear war less likely and thus aided "unilaterally assured survivability."[25] Although some Soviet experts differed about the extent of destruction in a nuclear war, none of their views excluded, and indeed most asserted, the desirability of nuclear-war-fighting capability, which they maintained furthered deterrence and made defeat less likely.

In addition, the Soviet analysis of the "correlation of forces" included all military forces—conventional as well as nuclear—plus nonmilitary factors—political, economic, and social—all of which were by definition caught up in dynamic change toward the "worldwide victory of socialism" and therefore made strategic as well as political stability unlikely as well as undesirable. Benjamin Lambeth well summarized the Soviet position:

> For the Soviets, "equivalence" and "balance" are unnatural because they imply an enshrinement of the status quo, something alien to every known tenet of Soviet political ideology and historical doctrine.[26]

In contrast, U.S. "balance-of-forces" analysis was usually quantitative and purely military. Moreover, MAD theory maintained that anything less than a complete first-strike capability was not destabilizing, except insofar as its critics maintained that it was, and therefore provided political advantage to the opponent.

However, Soviet doctrinal writings indicated, and Soviet conduct confirmed, that Moscow's view was the opposite—that is, massive Soviet strategic nuclear power energized Soviet decision makers, inhibited U.S. ones, increased the perception of other powers that the USSR must be taken very seriously because it was too strong and too willing to use its strength to be defied with impunity, and thus produced significant and increasing Soviet political gains.

Moscow consistently maintained that détente had to be accepted by Washington because the correlation of forces had changed to Moscow's favor. Rising Soviet military power thus resulted in a situation, as Soviet Foreign Minister Gromyko described it, in which "the present marked preponderance of the forces of peace and progress gives them [the USSR] the opportunity to lay down the direction of international politics."[27]

Soviet policymakers had other reasons for rejecting the views of U.S. arms controllers. Soviet analysts denounced U.S. nuclear-war-fighting theories and maintained that U.S. limited nuclear-war strategy plus nuclear-crisis bargaining were intended to prove political-pressure potentialities to Washington. Soviet experts and leaders had a historically conditioned belief in U.S. technological superiority. They also feared that recent U.S. military technological breakthroughs had started a U.S. drive to recover nuclear superiority.

Behind these views were psychological and historical differences between the United States and the USSR. First, the numerous and destructive invasions of the USSR predisposed any Soviet state to emphasize defense more than the basically untouched United States. Second, post-1945 U.S. strategic analysts were mostly scientists, mathematicians, and economists, with few historians or active-duty officers. Soviet strategic analysis, in contrast, were almost entirely professional officers. Very few Soviet civilians wrote about strategic problems. (Some of the latter did emphasize the danger of nuclear catastrophe more than nuclear-war-fighting capability.)

Many U.S. analysts maintained that because the Soviet strategic nuclear buildup would soon require conservative U.S. planners to assume that Minuteman ICBMs had become theoretically vulnerable to a Soviet first strike and, conversely, because massive mobile ICBM (MX) deployment (far greater than was then proposed) would require their Soviet opposite numbers to assume a U.S. first-strike capability, both sides' land-based missiles would thus be perceived to be strategically vulnerable. (Both sides' sea-launched ballistic missiles [SLBMs] and, to a lesser extent, bombers would not be.) Nevertheless, even partial mutual first-strike vulnerability logically challenged MAD theory because a first strike could make the destruction of the other side's nuclear-response capability so great that the destruction suffered by the side that launched a first strike could be less than sufficiently destructive to deter it from the first strike. Senator Moynihan provided MAD's epitaph:

> But the enterprise failed. And why? Because the Russian situation is not our situation, the Russian experience not our experience. If intellect must fail, let it fail nobly; and it is in nobly rejecting the notion of failure that intellect fails most often.[28]

Priority for Security and Nuclear-War-Fighting Capability

In 1980, some U.S. strategic analysts, notably Richard Burt, set forth the following case against priority for arms control.[29] Recently, primarily U.S. advances in weapons technology, notably warhead-delivery accuracy, greater verification difficulties, blurring of the traditional distinctions between nuclear and conventional and among strategic, Eurostrategic, and tactical weapons (especially by the multiple configurability of CMs), plus Moscow's strategic buildup and Third World expansion theoretically endanger both sides' nuclear deterrents. U.S. land-based missiles' vulnerability to a Soviet counterforce first strike in the mid-1980s—that is, "clinging parity"—will produce a Soviet "window of opportunity" in terms of the perceived vulnerability of the Minuteman and, therefore, will lower the credibility of U.S. escalation dominance.[30] Moreover, this effect will occur when the United States, and a fortiori its allies, will be so decisively dependent upon oil from the Persian Gulf that that area will be more vulnerable, due to increased local instabilities, to Soviet conventional predominance. U.S. extended deterrence (covering Western Europe and Japan) is also menaced by Soviet modernization of theater nuclear weapons, doubtful NATO LRTNF deployment, and West European views, as a result of the Soviet buildup, that the United States is losing not only superiority but also parity, plus the U.S. image of economic decline and governmental crisis.

These developments, arms-control critics maintained, require a major U.S. strategic and conventional buildup of a new kind. Given nuclear parity, and because of it, the strategic buildup should emphasize, rather than the (impossible) recovery of strategic superiority, hard-point attack and defense capability and management of a prolonged nuclear war through improved C^3I, nuclear redundancy and survivability, post-nuclear-attack deterrence, and space attack and defense—what Burt called "escalation agility" rather than "escalation dominance." Conventional buildup should involve large-scale CM and PGM deployment and an effective rapid-deployment force (RDF) for use primarily in the Middle East. Finally, strategic and conventional forces should be much more integrated in their doctrine strategy and escalation contingency planning.

Conversely, the argument went on, arms control has become not only irrelevant because it cannot respond to the new technological developments and security threats but also positively dangerous for it has impeded mobile-missile and hard-point-defense deployment; reinforcement of Indian Ocean deployments; and arms transfers to, and relations with, U.S. allies, notably by the SALT II protocol's limitation of CM range in Europe. However, arms control can reduce uncertainty and increase predictability by codifying, but until now not reducing, arms levels and therefore can facilitate the necessary unilateral U.S. arms buildup that must take priority over arms control.

How did the arms controllers reply? The United States was ahead of the USSR in military technology, they maintained, and had a significantly greater proportion of its nuclear forces in sea-based deterrents, which are for geographical and technological reasons less vulnerable to any ASW technology than the Soviet equivalent. These were facts that must be taken into account although they might not outweigh the greater proportion of the U.S. population in urban centers who are therefore more vulnerable to nuclear attacks.

Some arms controllers had become disillusioned with arms control, frequently in direct proportion to their mastery of the new technological developments. Indeed, something of an expert consensus developed in the United States about the impact of the new technological impediments on arms control. What did not develop, and seemed unlikely to, was any consensus about the importance of the political and humanitarian aspects of arms control: the avoidance of nuclear destruction and the furthering—or, better, resuscitation—of détente with the USSR.

Finally, some arms-control critics felt that the leaders of both sides were so extraordinarily reluctant to contemplate any use of nuclear weapons that too much concern about them, including about arms control, distracted attention from the much more-serious problem of the conventional military balance.

Some U.S. opponents of priority for arms control proposed that the United States should deploy a hard-point defense of its fixed land-based-missile silos,[31] even if this meant denouncing or renegotiating the ABM treaty; begin civil-defense preparations; and build up U.S. strategic, Eurostrategic, and conventional forces so that the Soviet window of opportunity would be as brief and nondestabilizing as possible and so the United States would have escalation dominance at all levels of nuclear-war-fighting capabilities.

The decline of support in the United States for arms control and MAD began in the early and mid-1970s. Indeed, by the end of his term, President Carter seemed simultaneously to be preaching priority for arms control and practicing the elaboration of a nuclear-war-fighting doctrine. Under the impact of these developments and arguments and of Soviet moves in Ethiopia and Afghanistan, he was persuaded[32] to sign a series of presidential directives (PDs) beginning in late 1978 that moved U.S. nuclear doctrine further along the multioption lines, ones that critics of arms control had been pushing since 1959, which had affected SIOP in 1961, and which had been pushed further by Secretary of Defense Schlesinger in 1973-1974. Presidential Directive (PD) 41 made it a civil defense aim to "enhance deterrence and stability."[33] PD 50 in August 1979 (after the invasion of Afghanistan) directed priority for security before arms control. It required that the United States not enter new arms-control negotiations unless and until the administration had thoroughly satisfied itself that such negotiations would not damage existing "defense and force posture goals," serve Western foreign policy interests and "restrain adversaries," and "limit arms competition and the likelihood of conflict." PD 53 directed development of C^3I; PD 57 called for intensification of mobilization planning; and PD 58 set up protection of the national command authority (NCA). Finally, PD 59 continued the evolution of a deterrent posture with emphasis on nuclear-war fighting; "countervailing" strategy including survivable C^3I, NCA, and reserve nuclear forces; and the targeting of a number of Soviet capabilities in addition to nuclear forces, C^3I, and political headquarters. The Reagan administration seemed likely to go further than its predecessor in these directions.

The European Connection

The East European Communist regimes had to continue to depend on the USSR for nuclear deterrence. Thus, one important effect of these military developments might be to increase, indirectly, their own defense burdens. A more-important one, however, especially for Romania and Yugoslavia, whose partial or complete independence from Soviet control had been furthered by détente, could well be that détente itself would erode further with resultant negative consequences for their independence. Moreover, with the exception of Prague and, partially, East Berlin, the other East European governments wanted and needed détente to get Western trade and credits to gain whatever autonomy from Moscow they could, so that they also found the erosion of détente alarming.

For Western Europe, the problems raised by the shift in the United States against priority for arms control was serious and frustrating. Economic giant but military dwarf, Western Europe wanted neither Cold War, double hegemony, nor Finlandization. It was thus permanently frustrated because it remained so much an object rather a subject of international politics. Two conflicting developments had been going on at the same time. On the one hand, Western Europe had become more doubtful of the credibility of the U.S. nuclear guarantee as the result of superpower strategic parity, but on the other hand, it had also become so accustomed to, and anxious to maintain, détente, even if only in Europe, that it psychologically used it to compensate for its fear of the Soviet military threat. Thus, Western Europe had been already in the process of diverging psychologically from the United States when the trend against détente and arms control in the United States was less than it had become by early 1981.[34]

This divergence was in considerable part the result of Western Europe's frustration for, on the one hand, it saw no security future without the United States, but on the other hand, U.S. policy seemed increasingly dangerous to it, by a combination that had no role to offer to Europe and in which both elements were contrary to its interests: either a double hegemony with the USSR, which restricted Europe's own security role by arms control, or defiance of Moscow in the Middle East at a time when the U.S. nuclear deterrent was weaker. West Europeans thought this so risky that they responded by trying to negotiate with Moscow themselves. Gaullism had been France's answer to this dilemma, and by early 1981 there were signs that some West Germans, and occasionally Bonn, were moving this same direction. Yet the United States would accept neither nuclear sharing nor Gaullism, and the Soviets would not accept Western penetration of Eastern Europe. Thus, Western Europe's frustration seemed likely to continue.

U.S. consultation with its West European allies was considerably closer during the SALT II than the SALT I negotiations. Moreover, the SALT II protocol's CM limitations were valid only for three years, and the Senate insisted that, even if SALT II were ratified, the protocol not be extended without its approval. West European public support for détente and fear of return to the polarizing cold war of the immediate postwar period, which would increase the security threat to Western Europe and decrease its autonomy vis-à-vis the United States, made Giscard, Schmidt, and Mrs. Thatcher endorse SALT II.

SALT I and II did not include forward-based systems (FBS)—that is, the U.S. nuclear-armed planes based in Europe and on carriers in the Mediterranean that could strike Soviet territory and the Soviet medium-range ballistic missiles (MRBMs) and Backfire bombers targeted on Western Europe. The Soviets maintained that U.S. FBS were strategic because they could strike the USSR. The United States maintained (and the USSR denied) that Backfire was strategic because it could reach the United States. At least until, and perhaps after, it agreed to negotiate LRTNF with the USSR, the United States was unwilling to negotiate on FBS with Moscow.

CMs had the most serious political consequences of these three weapons systems because they blurred the distinction between strategic and theater and between nuclear and conventional weapons since they can be (unverifiably) configured in combinations of these four modes.

The major Western European powers, collectively or even individually, were capable of developing CM technology fairly rapidly. CMs therefore offered for the first time the technological possibility to the West European powers to counteract somewhat their inferiority vis-à-vis the USSR this time, in contrast to the U.S. one- or two-key tactical nuclear weapons acquired in the late 1950s, with weapons systems entirely under U.S. control.

CMs were both less and more important for West Germany than for Great Britain and France: less because West Germany was barred from configuring them in a nuclear mode and therefore could not use them effectively as strategic weapons—that is, to target the USSR and more because West Germany could smother the Soviet forces and deployment areas in East Germany and Czechoslovakia with conventional, small, extremely accurate CMs. West Germany had far more geographic incentive to deploy CMs in this fashion than France or Great Britain .

There were some indications that the British and French already intended to acquire CM capability. The West Germans, some reports indicated, were also considering it. Not surprisingly, therefore, the USSR insisted in the SALT II negotiations that the United States undertake, by the "noncircumvention clause," not to transfer CM technology to its allies.

The CM problem was more complicated still. Some West Europeans objected that because the United States had agreed to limit CM technology in the SALT II protocol, it would be unlikely to reverse this. However, by early 1981, Senate ratification of SALT II seemed very doubtful indeed. Thus, extension of the protocol beyond 1981, when it would expire in any case, was even more doubtful, and U.S. CMs could not be deployed in Western Europe before then anyway. Discussion about CMs was still about a future, not a present, technology.

SALT as a negotiating framework had thus become intellectually obsolescent. Strategic CMs would make the problems of verifiability insurmountable. (Indeed, some people maintained that CM unverifiability, and therefore the enormous advantage they give the defense, stabilized, not endangered, the balance of terror.) Calibrating even rough parity was so complex that it became an increasingly important obstacle to arms-control negotiations. While one could argue that CMs in Europe would be simply more-effective replacements for FBS and Soviet MRBMs, and SALT I excluded both, the difference between FBS and MRBMs and CMs became very great. The argument for Washington's not negotiating away CM technology transfer to its allies in SALT was, therefore, that if the United States was to support NATO, it could not afford to appear to its allies to prevent them from deploying CMs, given the CMs' appropriateness to their military needs.

Western Europe felt increasingly menaced by the Soviet military buildup, notably SS-20 deployment. If the United States did not compensate for them, many conservative West Europeans saw Finlandization looming around the corner. If the United States did, however, many West European leftists felt, détente would give way to renewed cold war in Europe as well as in the Third World. European conservatives and leftists saw that two new factors would increase West Europe's military inferiority vis-à-vis the superpowers: (1) the increasing complexity and cost of weapons systems and Europe's dependence on Middle Eastern oil and its impotence to insure alone its own supply of it. Western Europe had thus become more dependent upon U.S. protection in an area, the Middle East, where Soviet military potential, given Soviet positions in Ethiopia, South Yemen, and Afghanistan, had increased, while U.S. military power there remained weak. Western Europe also disagreed with U.S. Middle East policy, which it saw as too pro-Israeli and too military oriented. Finally, as we shall see in a moment, for the Social Democratic Party (SPD) in West Germany, particularly for its left wing, for which arms control was the key motor of détente and therefore a precondition for the success of Bonn's eastern policy (*Ostpolitik*), the U.S. decline of interest in arms control struck at one of their priorities and made them reconsider their reluctant support for LRTNF deployment.

This was not the only West German frustration. Paris, given its geographical position, nuclear force, intervention force (used, for example in Zaire in Shaba II), and its nonparticipation in arms-control negotiations, could afford to be less concerned about U.S. (and Soviet) arms-control policies. However, Bonn was frustrated by the partition of Germany. It had the Red Army on its eastern border. It was economically sounder than the United States as long as its energy sources were assured but dependent on the United States for its nuclear umbrella, troop presence, and West Berlin.

Western Europe was also frustrated by the rapid shifts in U.S. policies on arms control and toward the USSR, defeat in Vietnam, Watergate scandal, and what West Europeans saw as its naive, dangerous, unpredictable, perhaps even ungovernable society. These impressions were greatly strengthened by the West European image of Carter's provincialism, indecision, and unpredictability, notably with respect to his last-minute reversal on the neutron-bomb issue. These impressions were further intensified by U.S. policy with respect to the Iranian Revolution and the Soviet invasion of Afghanistan, which led to the most serious U.S.-West European crisis since 1945.

Many West Europeans were becoming even more concerned about the policies of the U.S. conservative critics of arms control for several reasons. First, these policies allegedly imperiled détente and arms control and thus threatened to overwhelm the European island of détente. Second, they allegedly threatened to decouple the U.S. defense of Europe from that of the United States itself because they made the United States more able to absorb a Soviet nuclear first strike and therefore less likely to deter a Soviet conventional attack on Western Europe by a credible nuclear strategy of massive response. Third, if both superpowers deployed effective hard-point missile defense, the British and French nuclear forces would either have to do the same or become even less credible than they already were because they lacked sufficient numbers and accuracy. If they did the former, however, it would either cost much more or they would become technologically and therefore politically more dependent on the United States to provide it.

The European social democratic and socialist Left had remained noncommunist, its views menaced Soviet orthodoxy in Eastern Europe, and its international activities had played a great role in frustrating Soviet and indigenous Communist policy in Portugal and in helping to set up and support the Portuguese and Spanish Socialist parties. It traditionally tended to be for détente and arms-control negotiations with the Soviets per se and for leftist anticolonialism, and its left wing even more so, so that it had built-in obstacles in competing with the post-1975 Soviet expansionism in the Third World and the Soviet military buildup.[35]

The U.S. criticism of arms control set forth previously began to have impact in Western Europe in 1981. The election of President Reagan made it the dominant school of thought in Washington. Increased differences of views between Washington and at least Bonn and Paris therefore developed on these issues, the more so because the Reagan administration, far from giving as much priority to the ratification of SALT II as Carter had, opposed it and seemed to West Europeans reluctant to renegotiate it.

Thus, Western Europe was estranged from the dominant U.S. views on vital aspects of alliance security and likely to become more so. U.S.–West European relations would likely suffer further as a result.

2

The Superpowers and European Foreign and Defense Policies

Soviet Policy in Europe

By 1947 Moscow had given up hope of the Communist parties' coming to power or remaining in government in France and Italy. Thereafter, Soviet military strategy in Europe centered, first, on lowering the risk to Soviet security of the U.S. nuclear monopoly, inter alia because it immobilized Soviet conventional superiority; second, on deploying Soviet MRBMs targeted on Western Europe in order, by holding Western Europe hostage, to checkmate U.S. ICBMs; third, on building up Soviet ICBMs at least to parity with the United States inter alia in order to erode the credibility of the U.S. nuclear guarantee to Western Europe; and finally, by modernizing Soviet MRBMs (SS-20 deployment) and conventional forces to build up the perception in Western Europe that NATO was militarily inferior in all arms and thus to gain more political influence and diminish U.S. influence in Western Europe.[1]

The Soviet political aims in Europe were, first, to cement the partition of Germany and thereby of Europe; then to get Western recognition of the Soviet sphere of influence in Eastern Europe, and particularly in East Germany; thereafter, to prevent or at least slow down West European economic and military unity, and especially to prevent West Germany from getting nuclear weapons; and in the long run, to lower and eventually end U.S. military presence in Western Europe, provided it was not replaced by West German military power. Maximally, Moscow hoped gradually to Finlandize Western Europe—that is, to diminish U.S. influence there and to replace it, as Moscow had in Finland, by a Soviet veto over its foreign policies and political leaderships.

In the 1970s, the German treaties and the Conference on Security and Cooperation in Europe (CSCE) Final Act marked Moscow's first major successes in its détente policy in Europe, for they recognized de facto the territorial status quo and institutionalized détente on the continent. Thereafter the USSR, which maintained that détente constrained only the "imperialists" (that is, the United States and NATO) and thus assured Moscow the status quo in Europe while it expanded its influence in the Third World, pressed for the Soviet right to be consulted about Western European policies—the first step toward Finlandization.

Once the USSR gained nuclear parity with the United States, Soviet motives shifted from holding Western Europe as a hostage toward transforming it into a zone of peace. When, after the invasion of Afghanistan, the United States intensified its competition with the USSR in the Third World, Moscow tried harder to

31

preserve Western Europe as an island of détente. Moscow did so also because, fearful of encirclement by China, Japan, Western Europe, and the United States, it was trying to break out preemptively in the "arc of crisis"—the Middle East and Southwest Asia—and thereby also gain the extra dividend of Western European dependence on Soviet benevolence, not U.S. protection.

In the late 1970s the USSR saw dangers and opportunities in Europe. The principal danger was what Moscow saw as the Carter administration's drive to reacquire strategic superiority. (This was not Carter's intention, but rising U.S. defense expenditures, particularly in R&D, could eventually result in such superiority.) (Given the centuries of Soviet technological inferiority to the West, the USSR has always been very sensitive to new U.S. weapons developments.) In Europe, Moscow saw this U.S. drive for superiority reflected in the decision to deploy LRTNF, which could strike Soviet territory with much less warning time than before and which, because in part stationed in the Federal Republic, would tie Bonn more closely to Washington and eventually might enable West Germany to get access to CM technology and even nuclear warheads.

The main Soviet opportunity was the strong desire of Paris and Bonn, after the Afghanistan invasion, to maintain Western Europe as an island of détente. Both then thought the Carter administration indecisive, incalculable, reckless, and therefore dangerous to détente. By 1981 Bonn began to see the Reagan administration as dangerous because of its harder line toward Moscow, and Mitterand, the new French President, began to differ with Reagan's Third-World policies. Both had state reasons for trying to maintain détente in Europe: for France, for example, to maintain maximum foreign policy maneuverability like de Gaulle had; for West Germany, to preserve the gains of *Ostpolitik*. Both aims required good relations with Moscow. Giscard, who met Brezhnev in Warsaw, and Schmidt, who met him in Moscow, showed that they did not necessarily intend to follow the U.S. lead, and Mitterand, although more suspicious of Moscow, resented Washington's criticism of his bringing communists into government. Moscow tried to exploit its limited common interest with Paris and Bonn to keep détente in Western Europe in order to move it gradually toward regular, institutionalized consultation with Moscow and mediation between Moscow and Washington.[2]

The Decline of Détente: A Danger to *Ostpolitik?*

Détente in Europe made its first great leap forward with *Ostpolitik*. When in 1980 détente became threatened, *Ostpolitik* did as well. In the view of many Western conservatives, most importantly in Washington, Bonn's continued pursuit of *Ostpolitik* made West Germany (unlike the United States, its irreplaceable protector) unwilling to meet the new Soviet threat outside Europe. *Ostpolitik* thus became more an object than a subject of international politics.

West German *Ostpolitik* was both a cause and a result of the post-1968 intensification of East-West détente in Europe. Beginning in 1969 and concluding with the signature of the West German–Czechoslovak treaty in 1973, Bonn and Moscow gradually shifted from their maximum toward their minimum objectives —that is, they abandoned destabilization for de facto acceptance of the status quo in Europe.

Globally, in the 1970s the Soviets wanted to intensify détente with the United States. In Europe they wanted the West to accept their sphere of influence in Eastern Europe, to contain the rising power of the Federal Republic, to keep Europe quiet while they were becoming increasingly absorbed with the Chinese, and to take advantage of the coming to power in Bonn in October 1969 of the Social Democratic-Free Democratic (SPD-FDP) coalition, the first postwar West German government prepared to recognize de facto the German Democratic Republic and the Polish western boundary on the Oder-Neisse line.

Although West German public opinion had been moving toward compromise with the East, Brandt won on domestic, not foreign, policy issues, and most of the Christian Democratic Party (CDU) and all of the (Bavarian) Christian Social Union (CSU) remained adamantly opposed to compromise with the East. Only Brandt's thin majority and his personal commitment made his *Ostpolitik* possible.

The German treaties had several major results. The first was greater West German trade with and technology transfer to the East. The second was massive flow of West German and West Berlin visitors into East Germany and repatriation of several hundred thousand ethnic Germans from Poland and the USSR. The third was the abandonment by the USSR and their East European allies of their concentration on anti–West German propaganda. The fourth was the international recognition of East Germany and the convening of the CSCE. The fifth, and for the three western powers the most important, was the defusing of West Berlin as a crisis area. (Ironically, the Berlin agreement also made Berlin and Germany much less the center of Soviet-U.S. competition and thus lessened Bonn's role in Western policy.)

In the short run, *Ostpolitik* was intended to help stabilize East Germany, but its long-range objective was to help change it *(Wandel durch Annäherung)* and thus to "maintain the substance of the nation" (Brandt)—that is, to obtain sufficient human improvements *(menschliche Erleichterungen)* in East Germany so that the idea of one German nation would be preserved, West German human contacts with East Germany would be increased, and thus the way would be kept open toward the eventual peaceful reunification of Germany. As subsequent events demonstrated, however, this could also destabilize East Germany. Not that Brandt wanted to do this; he wanted such gradual change that it would slowly liberalize East Germany but not so alarm Moscow that it would reverse the process.

The potential for destabilization was evident to East Berlin, which was determined to resist it just as it had tried to block the treaties. Moscow also resisted it although it had removed Ulbrecht to prevent him blocking the treaties. Thus, détente between Bonn and the East initially produced relaxation of tensions among Moscow, Warsaw, Bonn, and Washington but also a combination of relaxation and irritation between Bonn and East Berlin. Brandt's hopes have not been fulfilled, nor were they soon likely to be. For although détente developed between West and East Germany and some state consciousness *(Staatsbewusstsein)* developed in the latter, it would be flying in the face of the lessons of history, notably that of partitioned Poland (1795–1918), to believe that national consciousness *(Nationalbewusstsein)* had developed, or soon would, in the smaller, weaker, poorer, Soviet-occupied and -dominated part of the Germany that as late as 1943 had ruled Europe.

East Berlin adopted a policy of *Abgrenzung* (delimitation) vis-à-vis the Federal Republic—namely, more-effective barriers against West German influence. This was Khrushcev's "intensification of the ideological struggle" with a vengeance, but if the East German Socialist Unity Party (SED) wanted to maintain its rule, and the Soviets their East German security glacis against the West, what alternative did they have? If Western visitors were not barred from Eastern Europe, its governments would not rot and topple. Hungary in the Soviet sphere and Yugoslavia outside it had showed that considerable Western tourism and travel abroad could be safely absorbed. However, Hungarians remembered the Soviet crushing of their 1956 revolution, and Tito enjoyed the legitimacy that came from leading a guerrilla victory against Hitler. East Germany was very different.

This difference became clear in the mid- and late 1970s. Reportedly, a hundred thousand or more East Germans formally applied to emigrate to West Germany. Many cited the CSCE Final Act as a justification. In 1977, most leading German writers protested East Berlin's deprival of citizenship to Wolf Biermann, a popular balladeer. Subsequently, some leading writers left, voluntarily or under pressure, for West Germany. An SED functionary, Rudolf Bahro, wrote a devastating attack on the East German bureaucracy and was imprisoned as a spy for his pains.[3] An anonymous group of SED cadres got the West German newsweekly *Der Spiegel* to publish their manifesto, notable for its personal attacks on the East German leader on Erich Honecker and his associates for their luxurious living and for its stress on German reunification.

This last incident illustrated the interaction between *Abgrenzung* and *Ostpolitik*. East Berlin in retaliation closed down *Der Spiegel's* East Berlin office, which had been opened as a result of *Ostpolitik*. Schmidt and Wehner tried to play down the whole affair for it threatened to interfere with their policy of negotiating with East Berlin rather than denouncing it. The CDU/CSU, conversely, demanded sanctions against East Berlin. These developments showed that *Abgrenzung* was necessary for the SED in East Germany, that it weakened support for détente in West Germany, but that most West Germans, given what they saw as its benefits—increased security and travel to East Germany—would continue to support *Ostpolitik* because they saw no alternative.[4]

As the post-World War II West German generation moved closer to power, guilt complexes decreased, patriotism increased, and economic power and political stability brought self-confidence and political reassertion. Giscard and Schmidt became for a while as close as Adenauer and de Gaulle. West German-U.S. relations worsened, but not decisively, because Bonn's security deficit was too great and only the United States could make it up. However, the national interests of Bonn and Washington were diverging with respect to policies toward economy, energy nonproliferation, the USSR, France, China, and the Arab-Israeli conflict. Many West Germans considered U.S. economic and energy policies indecisive and incompetent; the 1979 sudden, anti-USSR shift in U.S. policy excessive; the U.S. attempt to break the West German–Brazilian nuclear agreement unfair and selfish; the U.S. pressure on Bonn to prefer Washington over Paris contrary to Bonn's interests; the U.S. tilt toward China a danger to détente in Europe; and the U.S. refusal, because of domestic politics, to force a solution of the Palestinian problem a danger to Bonn's energy supplies. Personal relations between Chancellor Schmidt and President Carter were not good.[5]

Ostpolitik influenced many of these issues. Its results modified the views of the West German foreign policy elite. The great majority of them, SPD as well as CDU/CSU and FDP, still believed that the U.S.-troop presence and nuclear guarantee were the only effective way to make up the West German security deficit and thus contain rising Soviet power. Otherwise they gave priority to relations with France and the European Economic Community (EEC) over support of U.S. foreign policy. Also, for most of them, increased interaction between West and East Germany was an important national achievement whose preservation should be one of the major aims of Bonn's foreign policy—as Fritz Stern put it, a necessity, no longer an option.[6]

This attitude became stronger in West Germany because German national consciousness *(Nationalbewusstsein),* the desire to preserve the substance of the nation, had by early 1981 become stronger in East and West Germany as a result of the extensive contacts between their peoples that *Ostpolitik* had made possible. (However, a dual German state consciousness *[Staatsbewusstsein]* had also become stronger.) Belief in, or determination for, German reunification in the near future was not greater because *Ostpolitik's* de facto recognition of East Germany by West Germany dramatized the extreme unlikelihood of reunification in any short timespan, but belief in its rightness may well have increased.

This unity of nation and plurality of states was normal throughout most of German history. All those who felt themselves Germans were very rarely united in one nation-state. The German nation and the German state usually existed as different entities, and the former covered a larger area than the latter. Nor should the sense of belonging to the German nation be thought of as nationalism or patriotism in the sense that this would be true of England or France, the great historic nations of Western Europe. However, by the end of the 1970s, the sense of belonging to the same German *Kulturnation* had risen in both Germanies.[7]

Ostpolitik after the Invasion of Afghanistan

Strong opposition existed in West Germany, as it did in the rest of Western Europe, to U.S. sanctions against the USSR in retaliation for its invasion of Afghanistan. This opposition centered in industry, which opposed any cuts in trade with the East, and in the SPD left wing, which wanted to preserve the gains of *Ostpolitik*. Wehner spoke of the Soviet invasion of Afghanistan as a "preventive measure"[8] and revived his opposition to LRTNF deployment.[9] Brandt said that a boycott of the Moscow summer 1980 Olympic Games, urged by Carter, would be "nonsense."[10]

Another factor increased West German opposition to U.S. policy on this issue—namely, the East German, Polish, and Hungarian attempts to persuade Bonn not to follow Washington. East Berlin, increasingly tied by Bonn's plan into the West German economy, tried to persuade Bonn that Honecker's cancellation, after the invasion, of Schmidt's planned visit to East Berlin was an initiative of Moscow, not its own.[11] East Berlin, Warsaw, and Budapest shared the desire of Bonn and Paris to limit as much as possible the effects of the Soviet-U.S. confrontation about Afghanistan on détente in Europe. Thus the small and medium states in Europe gave higher priority to the maintenance of détente there than did either superpower.

The CDU/CSU denounced Schmidt for worsening West German–U.S. relations by not reacting more strongly against the USSR, a policy that, its chancellor-candidate Strauss maintained, was in the West German interest as well. Part of this was electoral politics (a new Bundestag was to be elected in October 1980), though, and Strauss himself made clear that he shared many of Schmidt's doubts about Carter's leadership.[12]

One might have thought that Schmidt's large 1980 victory would have given him ample leeway to repair Bonn-Washington relations with the Reagan administration, as indeed he wanted to do. However, by mid-1981 the SPD was more disunited than before, in part on foreign policy issues that made it more difficult for Schmidt to achieve this goal. To understand this, one must return to West German domestic politics.

First, Schmidt's 1980 electoral victory was primarily personal. The SPD did not do well, and its left wing was perhaps doubled to about a quarter of its Bundestag members. The FDP did very well. The CDU/CSU, although it lost, got its second highest percentage of votes in the history of the Federal Republic. Second, because the FDP did so well, and its right wing was conservative in economics, the tension within the governing coalition was greater. Schmidt's popularity remained very high, and on some issues, as we shall see, he almost seemed to be ruling against much of his own party and with the CDU/CSU. Third, and most important, the West German economic situation worsened sharply. There was a negative growth rate; over 6 percent unemployment; a major budgetary deficit; a $28 billion foreign-trade deficit, in part due to the second round of sharp increases in oil prices; and a sharp decline of the mark, accentuated by the rise of the dollar. Fourth, alliance relationships remained a problem for Bonn. Not only did the new Reagan administration, despite its desire to improve the style of their relations, suspect Bonn, on the Soviet issue, even more than Carter had, but also Giscard, in part for electoral reasons, took a somewhat harder line against the Soviets than Schmidt did. (So, largely, did Mitterand, with whom Schmidt's personal relationship was not close.) Fifth, the troika that had long led the SPD—Schmidt, Brandt, and Wehner—had fallen out with each other. Sixth, the CDU/CSU, rid of Strauss's chancellor candidacy, moved back toward the center, its leader, Kohl's, position greatly improved, and its unity became greater.

The main areas in which Schmidt came into conflict with his own left wing were nuclear energy and foreign policy. Both had in common a tendency toward pacifism—that is, the "Scandinavianization" of Europe. (This tendency went much farther in the Benelux countries and in Scandinavia itself.) Opposition to nuclear energy practically stopped the construction of nuclear power plants in the OECD countries, except France and Japan. If that opposition remained so effective in West Germany and the United States, both would remain dangerously dependent on OPEC oil.

The foreign policy issues were détente, defense expenditures, arms exports, LRTNF, and U.S. policy in El Salvador. The Reagan administration was much less sympathetic to détente than Carter had been, while the SPD remained determined to pursue *Ostpolitik* and its left wing (as we shall see later) to reopen the NATO LRTNF decision. Bonn cut back on projected rising defense expenditures, but Washington increased them greatly. The SPD left wing opposed West German arms sales to Chile and Saudi Arabia. (Schmidt favored all three.) They also denounced Reagan's increased military aid to the junta in El Salvador. There the USSR, Cuba, and Vietnam were aiding the guerrillas, while the Socialist International, including the SPD, through the latter's government-financed arm, the Friedrich Ebert Stiftung, was aiding the guerrillas' political arm, including the head of the small El Salvador Social Democratic party, but the CDU was aiding the Christian Democrat-headed junta through its foreign policy arm, the Konrad Adenauer Stiftung.

Thus, *Ostpolitik* again irritated Bonn's relations with its principal ally, the United States. In 1971, many people in Washington shared the doubts about *Ostpolitik* that Kissinger had expressed in the early 1970s, while Schmidt, like Adenauer—although for the opposite reason: support of, not opposition to, détente—had reservations about Washington's renewed hostility to Moscow.

The basic difference between Bonn and Washington in the late 1970s and early 1980s was that Schmidt (and probably most West Germans), although they shared the U.S. concern about Soviet advances, had a much greater stake than Washington in détente, lacked confidence in U.S. leadership, distrusted its style, and had three different emphases in national interest: toward East Germany, the USSR, and France. For most West Germans, closer, primarily humanitarian ties with, and more economic and cultural influence on, East Germany had become a German national interest. Schmidt had become pro-French. Thus Giscard's initial determination not to be pushed back into a cold-war-type subordination to U.S. leadership because of Afghanistan was another barrier to Schmidt's support of harder-line U.S. policies against the USSR. Rising West German self-confidence made automatic support of U.S. foreign policy less likely.

Meanwhile, a leftist, Protestant, pietist, pacifist wave was rising in West Germany as it was in the other Protestant countries of northern Europe. (Catholic France, Italy, and Spain seemed largely immune.) There had been others before and there would be others again. This one, however, had three new characteristics: (1) It was against both nuclear energy and nuclear weapons—that is, it was both ecological and pacifist; (2) it was the first such wave when a center-left government was in power in Bonn; and (3) it drew on the German Left's revulsion at the Vietnam War, Watergate, the so-called new U.S. cold war, its fear of war and of Soviet military power, its belief that the nuclear arms race was out of control; German intellectuals' historic fear of the corrupting influence of U.S. mass culture; and a renewed search for a specific German identity. This new wave was, in short, hostile to U.S. foreign policy and culture. It was not in theory neutralist for the Red Army was too close and West Berlin too isolated for that. Rather it was against (or between) both superpowers. It was violently opposed to LRTNF modernization. It maintained (or wanted to believe), that PD 59's nuclear-war-fighting strategy was more dangerous to Bonn's security than Soviet SS-20 deployment and that U.S. strategy was to make Europe, not North America, the scene of any nuclear war. It advocated unilateral West German initiatives to cut its military budget, and wanted to preserve détente in order to keep the key German gain from *Ostpolitik*—more-human ties with East Germany.

Thus, this leftist wave was not nationalistic but pacifist, European, and internationalist. But it was only a minority in the SPD and would in all likelihood remain so. It had no working-class base. Its primary inspiration was romantic, Calvinist, and pietist, not Marxist. However, its arguments could be, and indeed had been, used by conservative German nationalists. It needed to be understood in the West only less than it needed not to be overestimated because it was indeed a search for lost times. West Germany was too modernized, democratized, stable and above all too fearful to follow its call.

Finally, to Paris and Bonn, Afghanistan seemed a less-pressing issue than it did to Washington. Although the Federal Republic imported a considerably larger percentage of its petroleum from the Persian Gulf area than the United States did, Bonn and (at first) Paris thought that the danger of further Soviet military moves in that direction was considerably less than Washington thought. They also gave more priority to influencing the Third World on the issue and less to confrontation with the USSR. Bonn wanted to prevent Soviet-U.S. confrontation in the Third World from endangering détente in Central Europe, which in its view would endanger the security of the Federal Republic and lose the gains of *Ostpolitik*. By early 1981, however, many conservative West Germans and Americans, which meant most of the CDU/CSU and the Reagan administration, thought that Bonn's determination to keep *Ostpolitik* alive made it anticipate Soviet and East German pressure and thus prevent itself from countering it.

However, West Germany's need for its alliance with the United States in order to make up its own security deficit and to secure West Berlin, plus its democratic and Western orientation and its prosperity, made a break with Washington very unlikely, whether about preservation of the gains of *Ostpolitik* or anything else.[13]

The 1980 Polish developments raised the specter of a possible Soviet invasion of Poland in order to restore firm Communist party control there, a move that would gravely threaten détente in Europe. (They also showed how much Bonn and Paris had overestimated the stability of Gierek's Poland.) In mid-1981, it was still unclear whether Brezhnev would feel himself compelled to invade Poland. If in the end he did not, he would not do so in part, although only secondarily, lest he lose the benefits that he had gained from détente and *Ostpolitik* and those he hoped to gain in the future. However, Bonn's initial unwillingness to cooperate with Washington to develop detailed joint contingency planning if the USSR did invade Poland showed how much Bonn remained determined not to endanger *Ostpolitik*. It remained so even after East Germany doubled the cost of West German visits, in part to help ward off the Polish infection. That Bonn's initial response was hardly more than rhetorical made some U.S. observers wonder even more how much Bonn would do if Moscow did invade Poland.[14]

Conversely, the new Reagan administration in Washington seemed likely, should an invasion occur, to retaliate strongly. Thus a Soviet invasion of Poland might well worsen Bonn-Washington relations further rather than reunite the alliance. If that were to occur, many observers in Washington would see it as a confirmation of their fears—unjustified, in my view—that Moscow was getting Bonn to play a mediating role between the two superpowers and thereby unwittingly to drift toward its own self-Finlandization.

Thus, *Ostpolitik,* West German–U.S. relations, and détente in Western Europe were in 1981 endangered by instability in the Third World and Eastern

Europe and by the resultant intensified competition between the United States and the USSR. It was unclear who would profit from it most, Washington or Moscow, Bonn or East Berlin, and how much *Ostpolitik* would suffer in the process.[15]

CSCE

Because the initial proposal for what became the CSCE was a Soviet one, the West, especially Washington and Bonn, were at first determined to have nothing to do with it. The initial Soviet aims were two: (1) minimally, to get multilateral Western ratification of Soviet hegemony over Eastern Europe and the division of Germany and to increase East-West trade and technology transfers; and (2) maximally, to use the CSCE (in which, Moscow at first proposed, only European states would participate) to disengage the United States gradually from Europe while limiting the rise of West German influence and to increase tensions in the Western alliance.[16]

Moscow first proposed a European security conference in 1954. It reinforced its effort in 1969, just before the negotiation of the German treaties. By then, however, the situation had changed greatly and Soviet aims had therefore become limited to their minimal ones. Global and European détente was intensifying, the Vietnam War was ending, and the U.S. rapprochement with China was under way. Most important, by the end of 1972 the West German-East German Basic Treaty had been signed, in part, like the other German treaties, because Bonn and later Washington had successfully established linkage *(Junktim)* between them and Western agreement to the CSCE.

However, because of his pessimistic estimate of its prospects, Kissinger remained skeptical about CSCE. He did not want it and only reluctantly agreed to it. Once the CSCE met, he wanted it to end as soon as possible. However, because of Senator Mansfield's pressure for unilateral U.S.-troop withdrawals from Germany, he had two reasons to agree to a CSCE: (1) to signal Washington's determination to remain involved in European affairs and (2) to use U.S. agreement to it to bring about East-West negotiations on mutual balanced troop withdrawals and thereby to counter Mansfield's pressure. Moreover, the Nixon administration embraced the Chinese connection and East-West détente. It also became convinced, after initial skepticism, that Brandt's *Ostpolitik* was defusing the German question, notably in Berlin. Thus the United States finally and reluctantly agreed to participate in the CSCE.

The main minimum West European objective in CSCE was to prevent the Soviets from eroding what West European unity the EEC had achieved. The West Europeans also wanted to compensate for rising Soviet military power and to encourage contacts with, and more human rights in, the USSR and Eastern Europe. West Germany was determined to hold open a legal option for the peaceful reunification of Germany. The smaller West European states and the European neutrals saw it as a chance for them to play a significant role in European politics.

Yugoslavia and Romania wanted to use CSCE to deter the Soviets from invading or putting irresistible pressure on them. Poland and Hungary may well have wanted to use CSCE to strengthen détente more than the Soviets, but if so, Soviet pressure kept them as loyally pro-Soviet as East Germany, Czechoslovakia, and Bulgaria.

During the long CSCE negotiations at Geneva, the Soviets (and their East European allies) and the nine EEC members played the main roles. The United States was largely passive. The nonaligned and the neutrals tried to assert themselves, with some success.[17] This was easier because the conference operated by consensus—that is, all decisions had to be unanimous.

The CSCE negotiations became a struggle between Moscow, which wanted the West to *ratify* the status quo and noninterference in internal affairs (baskets 1 and 2) and to increase East-West trade, and the EEC states, which with some, but not strong, U.S. support pushed for increased East-West contacts and guarantees for human rights (basket 3)—that is, *change* of the status quo. From the Western viewpoint, CSCE's most positive aspect was the successful daily coordination of the policy of the EEC states for the first time through their then recently established political-coordination mechanism and their collective as well as individual signature on the Final Act—just the opposite of what Moscow had hoped to achieve in the conference.

The CSCE Final Act was inevitably a compromise that East and West could —and did—quote and use for their own purposes. The Soviets accepted provisions in basket 3 (on human rights) that they probably later regretted. Moreover, although the Final Act reaffirmed the territorial status quo, the same reservation was added to authorize the peaceful change that had been in the German treaties—that is, the Final Act made no legal change in the already existing situation. The Soviets could cite basket 1 to justify their rejection of any interference in their internal affairs and therefore to refuse to implement basket 3 to any major extent.

The West's fears about CSCE were not realized. CSCE neither inhibited Western defense expenditures (which the Soviet military buildup insured), discouraged Eastern Europe, nor interfered with *Ostpolitik* or West European integration, which it encouraged by its example of the first regular, successful EEC foreign policy coordination.

The Final Act provided for a review conference in Belgrade in 1977. This follow-up procedure had originally been pushed by the Soviets, who hoped thereby to be able to influence Western affairs while preventing Western influence in their own sphere. At first the United States opposed follow-up because it feared that the USSR would achieve these objectives. However, as CSCE went on and the EEC states became confident that they were making progress

on basket 3, the USSR became correspondingly less interested in institutionaliz-
ing the conference and thus modified their proposals to take into account the
initial Western objections to them. The military aspects of CSCE were reduced,
by the separation of M(B)FR from it, purely to confidence-building measures
(CBMs) such as mutual notification of, and exchange of observers at, military
maneuvers.

When the CSCE Final Act—it was not a treaty binding in international law—
was signed in Helsinki in 1975, much criticism arose in the United States and
Western Europe that the West was thereby ratifying the division of Europe and
Soviet domination over its Eastern half. Later events in the USSR and Eastern
Europe, however, showed that the Final Act encouraged dissidence and there-
fore became an embarrassment to the Soviets, not to the West. Moreover,
Helsinki and the Final Act, plus the subsequent Soviet and East European intensification of repression, further sensitized Western public opinion to this repression and therefore made it more skeptical about détente. Soviet and East
European dissidents tried to use the Final Act vis-à-vis regime pressures against
them. Many of the perhaps 100,000 East Germans who applied to emigrate to
West Germany cited the Final Act as justification. As was to be expected, however, the USSR and its East European allies, even Yugoslavia, on balance increased their repressive measures against dissidents.[18]

The Belgrade and Madrid CSCE Follow-Up Conferences

No one was surprised that the 1977–1978 Belgrade follow-up conference produced a final communiqué that essentially recorded that the conference had
come to no conclusion except to convene another follow-up conference in
Madrid in 1980. The basic reason for this failure was that Soviet and U.S.
policies with respect to the Belgrade conference, compared to what they had
been at the CSCE itself, had changed before Belgrade began. Soviet-U.S. détente
had steadily eroded. Washington, spurred on by U.S. public opinion, was increasingly disturbed by the Soviet military buildup and by Soviet activities in the
Third World. Moscow was concerned about the impact of the CSCE Final Act
in Eastern Europe and among Soviet dissidents and was infuriated by the beginnings of Carter's human-rights policy and the attacks by some West European
Communist parties on Soviet repression of their dissidents. The Soviets thought
Carter was unpredictable and therefore dangerous. They thus adopted at Belgrade
a "damage-limitation" strategy—that is, they refused to discuss any violations of
human rights (as set forth in basket 3 of the Final Act) and tabled other, mostly
disarmament, proposals. Their maximum proposals, an agreement on no first
use of nuclear weapons and no expansion of existing alliances (for example, not
allowing Spain to enter NATO) got, as they must have expected, nowhere.

The United States also reversed its position. While at Helsinki, under Kissinger's instructions, it had lagged behind Western Europe in pushing human rights, at Belgrade, led by the new U.S. delegation head, Arthur Goldberg, the United States pushed human rights much more aggressively. Goldberg, heading a delegation of over seventy representatives, including members of all kinds of U.S. minorities, often seemed to be talking more to a domestic U.S. audience than to the conference itself. The West Europeans were caught in between, far closer to the U.S. than the Soviet position, but they found Goldberg's tactics trying and sometimes counterproductive.

The Belgrade follow-up conference demonstrated, first, that all its participants wanted another follow-up conference or, more accurately, did not want to be held responsible for not having one; second, that Soviet and U.S. flexibility had become very limited because détente had become more limited, in part because of CSCE; and third, that given the probability of future crises in East-West relations (Western response to the SS-20, Soviet activities in the Third World, and so on), future follow-up conferences were unlikely to make much more progress than the very little Belgrade had achieved.[19]

Indeed, given the post-Afghanistan crisis in Soviet-U.S. relations, the fact that the Madrid follow-up conference met at all, and that the M(B)FR negotiations continued in Vienna, was a reassurance to some of the West Europeans and to the Soviets that Western Europe could remain something of an island of détente.

The preliminary agenda negotiations for the 1980–1981 Madrid conference[20] were longer and more difficult, and the level of East-West polemics was even more intense than at Belgrade. The negotiations centered on Afghanistan and the possibility of a Soviet invasion of Poland. The conference also had CBMs and the French pan-European conventional-disarmament proposal (CDE) on its agenda. The fact that the conference met and that the Western position at it was essentially uniform showed, along with the continuation of the stagnant M(B)FR negotiations, that Europe was indeed managing to remain an island of détente in the midst of greatly heightened Soviet-U.S. competition in the Middle East and Southwest Asia. In mid-February 1981, the United States endorsed the French CDE proposal, which Paris had modified in December to add a preliminary CBM phase, including mutual prior notification of military maneuvers from the Atlantic to the Urals. Brezhnev later accepted the French plan in principle but wanted an unspecified amount of more territory, presumably in North America, to be included in it. Later Moscow proposed, which the West refused, that at least the Atlantic be included. The U.S. endorsement seemed to have been an initiative of the Reagan administration to improve relations with the West Europeans in general and France in particular. It appeared to indicate that, as at Helsinki and Geneva and more than at Belgrade, the Madrid session might end up strengthening Western coordination and having France again involved in disarmament negotiations. It also showed, with it and M(B)FR still installed in mid-1981, that CBMs were one of the least common denominators of détente in Europe.[21]

M(B)FR

The M(B)FR negotiations were a 1968 Western initiative.[22] The Soviets first reciprocated in 1971. The United States had two main reasons for proposing the negotiations: (1) to try to diminish the Soviet asymmetrical military advantage on the Central European front and (2) to head off Senator Mansfield's pressure at that time for unilateral U.S.-troop reductions there. Washington successfully made Soviet agreement to M(B)FR negotiations a precondition for U.S. agreement to CSCE.

The other major Western power concerned, West Germany, wanted to avoid unilateral U.S.-troop withdrawals and to prevent the Soviets from getting any influence or control over the size and armament of the Bundeswehr. Bonn's strategy was therefore one of damage limitation. The French refused to participate. They wanted to avoid any international agreements limiting their military independence and any reduction, unilateral or otherwise, of U.S. military strength in Europe, which would lower their own security and therefore their military independence. In fact, the West's M(B)FR strategy gave priority to constraining the Soviets and keeping U.S. troops in Europe rather than to reducing military forces there.

The West also wanted to maintain alliance cohesion and levels of defense expenditures (which détente threatened to erode) and to avoid lowering U.S. deterrence credibility and increasing the rising Soviet threat to NATO's flanks by Soviet troop redeployment. (Increasing Soviet naval deployments and assertiveness in the Norwegian Sea[23] and the threats to Western security from the Iranian Revolution and the political-economic crisis in Turkey plus the Greek-Turkish dispute over Cyprus made these very real NATO concerns.) The 1979 Guadeloupe agreement among the United States, the United Kingdom, France, and the Federal Republic that Bonn would take the lead in an economic rescue mission for Turkey further increased Soviet concern about rising West German power.

The Soviets accepted M(B)FR in exchange for Western acceptance of CSCE and because they also feared a major unilateral U.S.-troop withdrawal that would be made up for by an expansion of the Bundeswehr and thereby a greater and less-U.S.-controlled military role for West Germany. Thereafter, they wanted, minimally, to insure that any U.S.-troop withdrawals from Europe would be symmetrical (so the Soviet military advantage would be maintained), gradual (not compensated for by increase, improvement in, or greater integration of West European and particularly West German forces), and therefore not politically destabilizing. Moscow rejected the Western demand that it acknowledge force asymmetry—that is, that the Warsaw Pact had more land forces on the Central European front than NATO did—because such an admission would repoliticize the issue of the presence of Soviet forces in Eastern Europe, which Moscow considered ratified by the Helsinki accords.[24]

Maximally, the Soviets hoped to participate in multilateral limitations and/or controls that would limit or prevent any increase in the Bundeswehr and thereby establish a Soviet *droit de régard* concerning it. Moscow wanted to preserve its asymmetrical military superiority in Europe; to get this ratified by the West; and to use M(B)FR to further détente, cut arms costs, and get Western technology and credits. By 1971, Moscow was deploying large forces on the Chinese border and wanted détente on its western frontier. The Soviets hoped also to further Soviet-U.S. bilateralism, thereby worsen NATO cohesion, slow down West European political and especially military integration, get U.S. forward-based nuclear systems out of Europe, and encourage a gradual U.S. military withdrawal from Western Europe that would not be replaced by a larger Bundeswehr.

M(B)FR negotiations began in 1973 in Vienna. It was agreed that the reduction areas should include the two Germanies, Poland, Czechoslovakia and Benelux. (Thus the Soviet Southern Group of Forces [SFG] in Hungary was excluded although it menaced Austria, Romania, Yugoslavia, and Italy.) Both sides initially expected political dividends from negotiations per se more than actual reductions.

The negotiations had produced no results by mid-1981. Moscow insisted (in fact, apparently, although no longer in theory) on symmetrical (unbalanced) reductions—that is, on preserving its superiority and on reducing foreign and indigenous forces and air and nuclear as well as land components, plus national subceilings (for example, on the Bundeswehr). The West insisted on collective asymmetrical (balanced) reductions in its favor in order, it declared, to get rid of the Soviet superiority in forces on the central front, with only ground forces involved and with no national subceilings. The West also proposed verified reductions of both stationed and indigenous forces and collective-strength ceilings for NATO and the Warsaw Pact. After a long deadlock, in December 1975 the NATO powers proposed their so-called Option III, which stated that not only ground troops, as they had until then insisted, but also some planes, missiles, and (largely obsolete) tactical nuclear weapons be reduced, something Moscow had been demanding. Thus, for the first time NATO was prepared to cut back on its military technology, which it had previously declared necessary to counterbalance superior Soviet troop strength. However, the West still insisted on asymmetrical reductions, to Moscow's disadvantage. In January 1976, the Soviets for the first time agreed to accept reductions only in stationed forces—namely, primarily Soviet and U.S. rather than indigenous ones, for example, West German—a position the West had consistently taken. However, the USSR still insisted that all reductions be symmetrical and that there be national-force subceilings (for example, for the Bundeswehr instead of only general East-West ones, as NATO insisted). In June 1976, Moscow for the first time gave figures on Warsaw Pact–force strengths (figures the West then and thereafter refused to accept as accurate) and proposed a second stage of small symmetrical troop and nuclear reductions of both stationed and indigenous forces. In April 1978, at West German initiative–Chancellor Schmidt, pressed by the SPD left wing, wanted to help revive détente–NATO proposed a slightly smaller Soviet tank withdrawal and no longer insisted that this affect Soviet forces in East Germany. In June 1978, the Warsaw Pact proposed an initial asymmetrical troop reduction of stationed (Soviet and U.S.) troops only (30,000 Soviet and 14,000 U.S.) plus the U.S. Option III in return for reductions of 1,000 Soviet tank and 250 armored personnel carriers (APC), a final common ceiling of 700,000 ground troops, and partially adjustable national subceilings (up to 50 percent of reductions by another ally). The Warsaw Pact still insisted that no state should increase its troop strength–that is, it demanded national ceilings in fact although not in theory. (However, the Bundeswehr was already up to its authorized ceiling in the 1954 Paris Agreements.) The Pact also proposed a common ceiling (700,000) and parity, thus abandoning its previous demand for national subceilings, but it still gave its troop strength at 805,000, while NATO estimated it to be 950,000; thus began the East-West "data-base" dispute that was still unresolved in early 1981.

In early 1979, in secret Soviet-U.S. bilateral negotiations,[25] Moscow proposed that Soviet and U.S. forces be reduced first and that West German and other European forces be frozen in size for two or three years until an agreement could be reached on their reduction as well.[26] The Soviets thereby accepted the Western position on this point. Moscow also agreed to discuss "associated measures"–for example, CBMs. However, no agreement was reached on the data-base issue, so the deadlock continued. Even so, Moscow began to indicate that the June 1979 SALT II signature (or, more likely, its ratification by the Senate) would enable more progress in M(B)FR, so prospects for agreement did not look entirely dark. On 6 October 1979, Brezhnev declared in East Berlin that the USSR would unilaterally withdraw 20,000 Soviet troops and 1,000 tanks from East Germany. (He did so primarily to try to block the pending NATO LRTNF-deployment decision.) In December 1979, the West proposed an initial cut of 30,000 in Soviet forces and 13,000 in Western, plus associated measures (CBMs and verifications).

These were only small steps forward. In mid-1981 agreement still seemed far away. Some changes in attitudes, primarily on the Western side, had occurred. Unilateral U.S.-troop reduction had become much less likely. Great Britain, rather than West Germany, came to favor cuts in indigenous forces. The West Europeans, particularly the West Germans, remained determined to prevent the Soviets from using M(B)FR to constrain their own political and military unity. The general Western malaise about détente lowered expectations. Incentives for agreement remained few because the conclusion of the German treaties and CSCE deprived the West of much of its linkage potential vis-à-vis the Soviets.

The Western critics of M(B)FR have raised three major objections:[27] one major motive for it, to block unilateral U.S.-troop withdrawal, is no longer pressing; its initial military premises, notably with respect to NATO-Warsaw Pact balance of forces and NATO warning time, are no longer valid because they have tilted drastically in Soviet favor; and its initial emphasis on manpower reductions never was valid and is less so now. M(B)FR's few remaining advocates, while largely agreeing with these points, stressed that in order to prevent the European theater military balance from tilting further in Moscow's favor, and because détente was so endangered outside Europe, M(B)FR negotiations should continue with priority on associated measures—notably, mutual inspection.

The M(B)FR's reduction area's military balance had indeed shifted in Soviet favor. U.S. official estimates were that since 1967—that is, during détente—the Soviets had deployed 154,000 more troops and 2,650 more main battle tanks in Europe, thereby invalidating NATO's three-week attack warning time required to fly U.S. troops from the United States and to redeploy U.S. troops in southern Germany to the north German plain. (The Soviets, incidentally, rejected these U.S.-troop estimates.) Soviet strategic parity, theater nuclear superiority, and conventional superior tank, artillery, and chemical-warfare technology were moving ahead of NATO's, as was Soviet-fleet and -submarine deployment, notably in the Norwegian Sea. Thus, the basic assumptions of NATO forward defense and flexible response—nuclear and qualitative conventional superiority plus adequate warning time—had disappeared for the Soviets had strategic nuclear parity, theater nuclear superiority, conventional parity and approaching superiority and also required much less warning time. Moreover, manpower levels were never a rational principal indicator of the theater balance for modern warfare is primarily decided by technology, surprise, and offensive initiative and doctrine, not numbers of troops. The initial U.S. motive, to ward off the Mansfield Amendment, no longer applied, and NATO alliance problems centered on increase in military expenditures and limits on East-West trade and no longer on the danger of allowing the USSR to "get a handle on the Bundeswehr." Finally, the center of the Soviet-U.S. confrontation and of Western vulnerability had moved from central Europe to the Persian Gulf, where the West was economically so vulnerable and conventionally so inferior that negotiations with the USSR, as the Indian Ocean talks showed, were counterproductive until the inferiority was redressed.

LRTNF

By mid-1981, the most important issue in West German–U.S. relations in Europe was the deployment by NATO of LRTNF[28] for CSCE was largely deadlocked, so was M(B)FR, and *Ostpolitik* was more influenced by LRTNF than vice versa.

Soviet military policy toward Western Europe during the last three decades had shifted from countering danger to exploiting opportunities in order to gain political influence there. It was inter alia helped to do so by exploiting the rise in Soviet weapons deployment. Once Soviet strategic parity with the United States was accepted in Washington as an organic component in the U.S. aim of strategic stability, the USSR began to modernize its Eurostrategic weapons (by SS-20 deployment) in order to increase the credibility of its deterrence of U.S. strategic nuclear superiority and thereby to prevent U.S. escalation dominance in Europe. The USSR also built up its conventional forces in Europe so that NATO became conventionally more inferior and more dependent on Eurostrategic and tactical nuclear weapons for deterrence. This occurred at a time when the U.S. strategic and Eurostrategic nuclear deterrent was also less credible because of the approach of theoretical U.S. Minuteman vulnerability, and the U.S. TNF in Europe became even more inferior to SS-20s than they had been to SS-4s and SS-5s before. The USSR also succeeded, in the SALT II protocol, in limiting U.S. CM range and, by agreeing to limit Backfire penetration of the United States, implicitly targeting it on Western Europe. The USSR was also modernizing its mobile medium-range ballistic missiles (MRBMs) by deploying SS-21 and SS-23, with ranges from 100 to 300 km., and the mobile LRTNF SS-22, with a 1,000-km. range. The latter were being deployed in western Russia, but if they were deployed in Eastern Europe they could reach Western Europe. The LRTNF discussion in NATO centered exclusively, and probably unwisely, on SS-20. However, if the West were to agree to include FBS in LRTNF negotiations, it would probably *want* Soviet MRBMs included as well.

These reasons were not the only ones that made the Soviets build up their nuclear forces. Given their initially inferior nuclear capability, it was easier in the 1950s and, as it turned out, sufficient for them to build IRBMs rather than ICBMs. Moscow thus built up its nuclear and conventional forces, but the West did not.

These actions could well be interpreted by the Soviets (and were by some West Europeans) as implicit signals that the United States could remain, like the USSR, a nuclear sanctuary while a nuclear war would be fought out in Europe. Thereby Western Europe could be decoupled from its U.S. strategic guarantee. (Conversely, the revival of the discussion in the United States about hard-point Minuteman defense could send the same signal to Moscow.)

The USSR argued that its strategic position was fundamentally different because, given its central geographic location, it needed to deter the U.S. ICBM and SLBM strategic forces; the U.S. FBS; and the British, French, and Chinese strategic forces, while the United States, Britain, France, and China needed to deter only the Soviet nuclear force. Therefore, Moscow argued, the USSR had to have nuclear superiority over the U.S. forces alone (an argument that Moscow had made in the SALT negotiations). The United States, however, could not accept what this would mean—namely, U.S. strategic inferiority to the USSR. Moreover, Moscow's SS-4s and SS-5s (targeted on Western Europe), like the U.S. Pershing IRBMs targeted on Eastern Europe, needed modernization. Moscow could much more likely prevent LRTNF modernization while frightening

Western Europe by massive SS-20 deployment than it could prevent the United States from keeping up with Soviet ICBM deployment, and by doing the former it would keep the United States in an inferior nuclear position in Europe. Finally, the Soviets felt that Eurostrategic superiority would enable them better to contain rising West German power. Moscow therefore began to deploy SS-20s.[29]

Soviet fears about LRTNF deployment, although deliberately exaggerated for foreign consumption, in part reflected genuine Soviet concerns. Moscow feared that sooner or later West Germany would get more influence over whatever LRTNF were deployed. Moreover, the West German–based LRTNF would for the first time be targeted on Soviet territory with a six- to eight-minute warning time for Moscow. (The U.K.- and Sixth Fleet–based U.S. FBS had long been targeted on the USSR, but they had never been based in West Germany and had a far longer warning time.) Finally, LRTNF was a product of major technological breakthroughs, especially in CMs.

NATO deterrence doctrine in Europe was in theory intended to deter Soviet nuclear first use. Given NATO's conventional weakness, however, it was in fact intended to prevent NATO's being self-deterred from credible nuclear first use in order to prevent conventional defeat. Thus Soviet strategic parity and Eurostrategic superiority lowered the credibility of NATO's deterrence posture and invited successful Soviet political pressure. In fact, Western Europe was condemned by its geographical proximity to the USSR (as compared to its distance from the United States) and by its military weakness (as compared to Soviet strength) to a worse fate than ever: to rely for deterrence on a U.S. response even when the United States had become vulnerable and was not attacked.

This was West Europe's dilemma because it had to want deterrence and détente; it had to want SALT and fear its results; it had to want a credible and invulnerable U.S. second-strike deterrent, but it had to fear that Washington would prefer a nuclear war fought in Europe; and finally, it both had to want LRTNF and to fear it.

In the late 1970s, Moscow was thus trying to get a handle on the U.S. FBS and to prevent CM deployment and U.S. transfer of CM technology to the Federal Republic. It had already established the precedent of CM range limitation by the SALT II protocol and, inferentially, by the SALT II noncircumvention clause. The 1979 NATO offer to negotiate on LRTNF in SALT III for the first time opened the way for the Soviets to demand, as they did, that FBS also be involved in SALT, which until then Washington had refused. Moscow also hoped to continue to profit from its vast geographical expanse, which maximized U.S. difficulty in countering Soviet SS-20 mobility.[30]

SALT II and Western Europe

West European concern about U.S. consultation with them during SALT II was less than with SALT I because Washington kept the NATO allies informed of the progress of the negotiations, and the allies could express their concerns about them. West European experts were concerned about three substantive issues: (1) that SALT II did not freeze Minuteman vulnerability and therefore endanger NATO's escalation credibility; (2) that the protocol's limitation on SLCM and GLCM range to 600 km. was not matched by any equivalent Soviet concession and would also make it difficult to prevent its incorporation in SALT III; and (3) that the Soviet interpretation of the noncircumvention clause, although rejected by the United States, represented a Soviet claim for a *droit de régard* on U.S.-West European military cooperation.[31]

The Western perception in the 1970s that the USSR had attained strategic nuclear parity with the United States, that it was moving toward an ICBM first-strike capability, and that the United States was not responding to Soviet SS-20 deployment produced a West European crisis of confidence in the credibility of the strategic (SIOP) and Eurostrategic (TNF) U.S. nuclear deterrents and of U.S. will, doctrine, and capability. The West Europeans questioned the credibility of a U.S. SIOP response to a Soviet theater nuclear strike—that is, of U.S. escalation dominance.

These developments highlighted the differences in U.S. and West European nuclear priorities. The United States wanted to keep the SIOP release threshold credible but high in order to enable flexible nuclear response and to prevent a superpower nuclear exchange. Western Europe had to make SIOP's involvement credible at a low threshold in order to deter a Soviet theater nuclear attack. Specifically, it had to prevent Moscow from believing that an initial nuclear exchange might, by implicit agreement with the United States, be limited to Western and Eastern Europe. (Logically, therefore, Western Europe should want MX as well as LRTNF deployment.) The United States, this West European argument continued, might agree that both superpowers would be nuclear sanctuaries because of strategic parity, U.S. Minuteman vulnerability, and NATO TNF inferiority. The last was true because U.S. tactical weapons in Europe were vulnerable to Soviet preemption, U.S. Pershing missiles could not strike the USSR, and the assignment of the Poseidon SLBMs to NATO was not credible either to the Soviets or the West Europeans since a U.S. president would be inclined to think of them as a part of SIOP and because a SIOP first or second strike would not necessarily or credibly destroy Soviet mobile SS-20s. Moreover, SS-20 greater accuracy and smaller yields were more favorable to Moscow in destruction-acquisition calculations than SS-4s and SS-5s had been.

The Soviets, conversely, wanted to confirm their strategic parity with the United States and maintain their current conventional and LRTNF superiority in Europe in order to push the West Europeans and especially the West Germans, given *Ostpolitik* and West Berlin's vulnerability, toward a mediating role between the superpowers and eventually toward self-Finlandization.

NATO's problem was, therefore, to contain, and if possible to reverse, the military effect of Soviet SS-20 deployment and thereby its political impact in

Europe. Because of the increasing complexity of MRBM and IRBM ranges, accuracies, and verification problems, East-West negotiations about them could well raise more problems than they would answer. The proposed negotiations would not include the British and French nuclear systems, the U.S. Poseidon SLBMs assigned to NATO, or U.S. land- or carrier-based FBS. The December 1979 NATO offer of LRTNF negotiations effectively extended the SALT framework to include what NATO had always before refused—FBS in Europe.[32] Nor, as subsequent events made only too clear, was West European support for NATO's LRTNF decision assured.

The military case against LRTNF deployments made by some Western experts was that the 572 additional warheads would not significantly change the overall Soviet-U.S. strategic relationship; that the Eurostrategic nuclear balance was only a part of the global nuclear balance; and that technological advances made U.S. ICBM, SLBM, and IRBM basing more cost-effective outside Central Europe. Some observers in Washington were therefore not initially very concerned about Soviet SS-20 deployment.

Indeed, the argument against LRTNF deployment continued, the SS-20 replaced only the SS-4s and SS-5s being withdrawn, and the Soviets had fewer launchers targeted on Europe than they had had a decade before. Moreover, to say that the SS-20 was mobile and had MIRVed, more-accurate warheads, this argument went on, and that therefore SS-20 deployment threatened the Eurostrategic balance, was unconvincing because the United States had greatly increased its warhead capability during the life of SALT I (through the new MK-12A warhead) and was still superior to the USSR in this aspect. For example, Pershing 2s could strike Soviet strategic nuclear capability with extremely great accuracy, within four to six minutes from their launching, while the Soviet missile flight time to hit U.S. hard targets was around thirty minutes.[33] The concept of a Eurostrategic balance based only on IRBMs, this argument concluded, also neglected U.S. nuclear-capable FBS and Soviet and U.S. nuclear-missile submarines assigned to European targets.

In my view, the essential justification for LRTNF deployment was political: SS-20 deployment, without a NATO reply, had already created, and would do more so in the future, a belief in Western Europe of growing Soviet superiority, that, if not countered, would serve the Soviet aim of moving toward Europe's Finlandization. Thus, that belief should be countered. Moreover, U.S. leadership in LRTNF deployment in Europe would reinforce U.S. troop presence there by convincing West Europeans that the U.S. strategic nuclear deterrent would not be decoupled from Europe as a result of credible Soviet belief that the United States might abandon Europe's nuclear defense in order to become a nuclear sanctuary from a Soviet attack. Finally, only LRTNF deployment would make possible successful Western Eurostrategic negotiations with Moscow.

It followed from the previous discussion, its proponents argued, that LRTNF deployment in Western Europe (not outside it, as was the case with MLF in the

1960s) was necessary to renew in Moscow and Eastern Europe the credibility of U.S. strategic and theater weapons, remove the threat of Soviet escalation dominance, and complement the restoration of the second-strike credibility of U.S. land-based missiles.[34]

By the end of the 1970s, NATO discussions therefore centered on LRTNF — that is, intermediate-range ballistic missiles (IRBMs) stationed in, and with ranges covering, Europe including the European USSR. Like the U.S. FBS, the Soviet MRBMs targeted on Western Europe, and the Soviet Backfire bomber, these weapons were not included in SALT or M(B)FR negotiations (hence the phrase *gray area*).

The previous U.S. and West German fumbling on ERW (enhanced radiation weapons, or the neutron bomb), and the massive Soviet conventional buildup on the central front, which was only partially compensated for by the NATO long-term-defense program, influenced Bonn and Washington to make LRTNF deployment the test of NATO's effectiveness in deterring a Soviet attack in Europe.[35]

The West European left, especially the left wing of the SPD, pleaded for negotiations with the USSR before, and hopefully as a substitute for, NATO LRTNF deployment. Indeed, the LRTNF controversy interacted with West German and particularly SPD politics as decisively as the SPD 1959 endorsement of NATO.

The conservative, neo-Gaullist desire for a larger West European role in Eurostrategic matters argued for a West European nuclear force. However, France resisted this from explicitly nationalist motives, Great Britain from implicit ones, and West Germany was pledged to remain nonnuclear. (The French nuclear force, although no longer *à tous azimuths*, was intended as much to guarantee Paris political parity with Bonn as to deter a Soviet attack.) The main West European and U.S. reason for LRTNF deployment was therefore political. Soviet SS-20 and Backfire deployment intensified the West European, particularly West German, fear of decoupling. This caused West Europeans to fear a Soviet limited nuclear attack on Western Europe and was in turn the major political reason why the United States and West Europe advocated LRTNF deployment.

LRTNF and West German Politics

The Federal Republic was militarily the most threatened by SS-20 and Backfire deployment because it was geographically closest to the USSR and also non-nuclear. However, its SPD-FDP government, and some of the CDU, also had a special interest in détente to preserve the gains of *Ostpolitik*, particularly the greater human contacts between West and East Germany.

The LRTNF issue was first brought to public attention by Chancellor Helmut Schmidt in a speech at the International Institute of Strategic Studies

(IISS) in London in October 1977. He reflected West German concern about the Carter administration's agreement with the Soviets to exclude Eurostrategic weapons from SALT II and to accept the protocol limitations on CM range and therefore, as Bonn saw it, ambivalence about CM-technology transfer. The issue was also discussed extensively in Franco-German meetings, which influenced Paris to move toward a more-European security policy and toward endorsing SALT II and Bonn to endorse the French European-disarmament proposal.[36]

In 1978, Schmidt strongly endorsed U.S. SALT II ratification for he feared that its rejection would imperil détente (and therefore *Ostpolitik*) and lower U.S. prestige and nuclear credibility. However, he rejected LRTNF deployment in the Federal Republic alone (singularity) because he felt this might repeat the neutron-bomb fiasco, be the first step toward the renationalization of West German defense policy, and thereby raise the specter of greater West German military (or even nuclear) strength, endanger the multilateral character of NATO, and create fears of West German domination of Western Europe.

The LRTNF issue became involved in the spring of 1979 with West German *Ostpolitik*. The left wing of the SPD, spearheaded (exceptionally) by Herbert Wehner, wanted to negotiate on the subject with Moscow before any LRTNF-deployment decision was taken.[37] Their motives were the traditional SPD priority for disarmament plus German nationalism—that is, their fear that LRTNF deployment would erode the gains of *Ostpolitik*, block rapprochement between the two German states and thus ultimate German reunification, and, Wehner may have believed, play into the hands of the Soviets. Behind this was the widely shared West German perception that the Federal Republic's geographical position and military vulnerability required détente with Moscow and West European unity plus continued security reliance on Washington. Thus, for the first time in twenty years, security and reunification were linked in SPD public discourse, and Wehner and the SPD left wing again advocated a policy (negotiations before deployment) parallel with Moscow's—although, I hasten to add, for quite different reasons.

In a 6 October 1979 East Berlin speech, Brezhnev announced a unilateral Soviet withdrawal from East Germany of 20,000 troops and 1,000 tanks and proposed immediate NATO–Warsaw Pact negotiations about (and before) LRTNF deployment plus, if they were successful, a unilateral Soviet cutback on SS-20 deployment. Otherwise, he threatened, Moscow would counter LRTNF deployment by further Eurostrategic deployment of its own.[38]

Brezhnev's objectives also probably included breaking the M(B)FR data-base logjam, but he primarily wanted to prevent LRTNF deployment. By autumn 1979, however, Wehner's attempt had been blocked by the majority of the SPD plus Genscher and the FDP (to say nothing of the CDU/CSU.) By December 1979, the efforts of Schmidt, Genscher, and the Carter administration had pushed through an SPD and then a NATO expert's proposal to produce and deploy land-based LRTNF weapons plus simultaneous negotiations between Washington and Moscow about mutual reductions of Eurostrategic and nuclear weapons.

By the opening of the SPD convention in West Berlin in early December 1979, an expert group had drafted such a leadership motion. It was somewhat, but not decisively, amended at the convention where Schmidt made clear that LRTNF was a question of personal confidence in him. Wehner, Brandt, and Bahr supported him. Since without him the SPD had no chance of defeating Franz Josef Strauss in the forthcoming 1980 parliamentary elections, the resolution, not surprisingly, passed with an 80 percent majority.

Meanwhile, the U.S. and West German efforts had run into serious opposition by the Belgian and Dutch left wing, even more among left-wing Christian democrats than left-wing socialists. (In part, these developments reflected the revival of the historic traditions of neutrality in both countries.) The Soviets propagandized extensively in West Germany, Belgium, and the Netherlands. Denmark and Norway, which anyway accept no nuclear weapons, also wavered. In Italy, where LRTNF were also to be stationed, the Italian Communist party, encouraged by its then partial rapprochement with the Communist Party of the Soviet Union (CPSU), actively opposed it, but the Christian democratic government pushed it through parliament. In sum, Latin, Catholic Europe was for LRTNF, but Protestant northern Europe was doubtful.

At the NATO ministerial meetings in mid-December 1979, the experts' recommendations were unanimously adopted. West Germany, Italy, and Great Britain supported them in toto. Belgium reserved its deployment decision for six months and the Netherlands delayed its for two years.

NATO thus decided to modernize its LRTNF potential by deploying 108 Pershing 2 missiles and 464 GLCMs, each with only one nuclear warhead, and simultaneously announced an offer for U.S.-Soviet LRTNF negotiations: within the SALT III framework, about land-based LRTNF only, step-by-step, on the principle of equality, and with verifiable results.[39] The negotiation proposal was primarily the result of political pressures in Western Europe, especially in the SPD and in Belgium and the Netherlands. It also took account of the fact that CM range was limited in the SALT II protocol, that putting the negotiations in the SALT process would help avoid decoupling, and that it would avoid any discussion of the British and French nuclear deterrents.[39]

The NATO communiqué also set specific conditions for U.S.-Soviet negotiations on LRTNF—namely, parity in, and adequate verification of, mutual LRTNF reductions, a special NATO consultative committee to assure full consultation with the United States on the negotiations, and unilateral withdrawal of 1,000 U.S. tactical nuclear warheads from Western Europe (a countermove to Brezhnev's unilateral-withdrawal proposal.)

The communiqué also included a new M(B)FR proposal—namely, withdrawal of 13,000 U.S. and 30,000 Soviet troops from Central Europe and greater mutual inspection of troop maneuvers. NATO also agreed to introduce at the 1980–1981 CSCE Madrid follow-up conference further CBMs concerning notification and observation of military maneuvers plus the French proposal for a European conventional disarmament conference, both to cover the area from the Atlantic to the Urals. Although the Soviets at first declared that they would not negotiate at all, it seemed probable that sooner or later they would so that they could try to slow down or prevent the LRTNF-deployment decision.

Carter's sudden, drastic reversal after the invasion of Afghanistan, which led, often with little or no consultation with Western Europe, to the U.S. Olympic boycott, grain embargo, and pressure on Western Europe to cut back on East-West trade, plus the overall West European image of his indecisiveness and unpredictability, and the rising fear of war in Western Europe led Giscard and Schmidt in early 1980, despite U.S. pressure, to talk to Brezhnev, separately, themselves. Before he met the Soviet leader, Schmidt hinted that if Moscow would freeze SS-20 deployment, some or all of LRTNF deployment could be postponed, but he abandoned this idea shortly thereafter.

Thus, in mid-1981 deployment of, and negotiations about, LRTNF remained unclear. Uncertainty about them, and the fate of SALT II, was increased by the election of President Reagan and the ambivalence, when not hostility of many in his administration toward arms control.

Yet both Washington and Bonn had become so committed to LRTNF deployment that the blow to NATO's credibility, and indeed to any prospect for negotiations about it, would be very great if deployment did not occur, while conversely the USSR seemed unlikely to reverse SS-20 deployment given the advantages in Europe (and vis-à-vis Beijing) that is had obtained from it.

By mid-1981 the anti-LRTNF movement in the Netherlands appeared victorious and, much more important, it was rising steadily in West Germany. There Schmidt's authority had also, in part for that reason, declined considerably. In addition, the SPD lost control of West Berlin and its Württemberg-Baden branch opposed LRTNF deployment. Then at the end of June 1981 SPD Chairman Willy Brandt visited Moscow, primarily to discuss LRTNF. Brezhnev basically repeated his moratorium proposal, which would freeze Soviet Eurostrategic superiority while accepting U.S. production of LRTNF, but not their deployment, during the negotiations. (Schmidt immediately rejected this proposal.)

Brandt's motives were complex: his deep desire to stop the arms race; Soviet threats of further escalation if LRTNF were deployed; his determination to integrate the growing anti-LRTNF movement into the SPD; his revulsion against what he saw as the Reagan administration's anti-arms-control posture; and his reviving personal ambition. What effect all this would have in West Germany remained unclear in mid-1981. Brandt's Moscow visit was a further indication that Moscow hoped at least to delay LRTNF deployment for a prolonged period if not indefinitely, primarily through manipulation of West German politics. His visit also increased Washington's distrust of the SPD, the more so because at the same time Brandt spoke favorably of a nuclear-free zone in Northern Europe, a longtime Soviet proposal which Washington and Bonn continued to oppose.

Brezhnev insisted that U.S. FBS be included in the negotiations, which meant not only F-111 planes stationed in Great Britain but also nuclear-armed carrier-based airplanes in the Mediterranean and Polaris and Poseidon SLBMs assigned to SACEUR. Soviet SS-20s were in part targeted against China, based in Siberia (that is, not in Europe), and perhaps two-thirds of them were retargetable from Europe to China and vice versa. Finally, and perhaps most seriously, the USSR was ahead of NATO in mid-1981, but NATO might draw ahead of it if its LRTNF decision, or more, were implemented despite the political difficulties in Europe of doing so. Thus, Moscow was being asked to surrender its advantage because of a future disadvantage that it might hope to avoid without successful negotiations. Judging by past history, the prospects were bad indeed.

By mid-1981 the prospects for continued support of LRTNF deployment in Western Europe were also not good. Belgium and the Netherlands gave only conditional approval to the NATO deployment decision. While Italy and Great Britain would probably continue to support deployment on their territory, Schmidt had been facing increasing harassment from his own left wing on LRTNF and other issues largely because of declining German prosperity. All these development were hardly likely to encourage the USSR to compromise with the United States on LRTNF.

Even so, by mid-1981, because of West German pressure, the Reagan administration proposed credible LRTNF negotiations. How credible these would be, however, given the appointments of several anti-arms-control officials in the new administration, remained to be seen.

3 Economics and Energy

with *John Van Oudenaren*

Military power is not the only thing that has international political impact. Economic strength—and weakness—has such impact as well. The more important technology becomes in military operations, the more their interrelationship becomes powerful. Each state's perception of the economic power of the other is bound to influence its estimate of its own and its opponent's military and political strength—what Moscow calls the correlation of forces. The more serious a competitor's domestic or international economic problems, the less of its attention and its budget may be devoted to military competition. Economic and energy problems also greatly influence the images of the USSR and the United States throughout the world, particularly among each's major allies and the major nonaligned countries.

The Energy Crisis

The most important economic event in Europe, North America, and Japan in the last decade was the quadrupling in 1973–1974 of OPEC oil prices.[1] The energy crisis had four major causes: (1) rapid, massive substitution of cheap oil for coal in the developed world (the post-1950 Western and Japanese boom was largely based on cheap energy); (2) the political independence of the oil-producing states, their resultant manipulation of the independent oil companies against the seven major oil companies, and then their use of OPEC to get control over oil supplies; (3) the loss of excess, primarily U.S. capacity; and (4) the dangers of rising instability in the oil-producing areas (as the Iraqi-Iranian War showed) to the price and security of the oil supply.

In retrospect, the West and Japan could not have expected to indulge indefinitely their appetite for cheap energy without controlling its supply. The energy crisis was a result of the retreat of Western power from the Third World, the loss of U.S. strategic and regional military superiority, the U.S. failure to bring about a settlement of the Arab-Israeli dispute, the decline in U.S. oil production, and the Iranian Revolution and the Iraqi-Iranian War. Even the United States, the least affected by these developments, paid fifteen times as much for the one-half of its oil that it imported in 1979 as it had in 1970 for the one-quarter.

Why, by 1981, nearly a decade after the 1973 quadrupling of oil prices, had so little been done to meet the crisis? For the usual reasons that democracies do

57

not face up rapidly to crises—namely, ignorance, complacency, whistling in the dark; the mistaken belief that solar energy could soon replace oil; the failure until 1981 to decontrol U.S. domestic oil prices; the ecologists' blocking (except in France) of nuclear power-plant construction and harassment of increased coal production—the most effective immediate countermeasures; and the reluctance of politicians, even those few who understood the nature of the crisis, to tell their electorates what the crisis was and to vote for drastic measures to meet it. On the contrary, Western publics believed either that no energy crisis existed or that the oil companies were to blame for it. Until 1979, the United States talked with the USSR about freezing naval deployments in the Indian Ocean rather than building up its naval and air strength there. Carter disastrously underestimated the political and energy impact of the rise of Islamic fundamentalism and its revulsion against the Western model of modernization.

The USSR did not create these problems for the United States and Western Europe, but it profited from them. It supported those radical elements in the Arab world, including Nasr and the Palestine Liberation Organization (PLO), which have, as Moscow wanted and expected, intensified Arab and Iranian hostility to the West and thereby the political destabilization of the Middle East. Moscow's invasion of Afghanistan put fighter-covered Soviet aircraft within 500 miles of the Straits of Hormuz and thus demonstrated to the Gulf oil states, to Moscow's foreign policy profit, the nearness of Soviet power and Moscow's capability and will to use it. By 1990, France and West Germany will depend on the USSR for 30 percent of their natural-gas supply. Although they will thereby diversify their energy supplies, at least in theory they will be more subject to Soviet political pressure. Even so, the instability in the Middle East oil states was fundamentally domestic in origin. They were far more Muslim than Marxist. Their instability was intensified by U.S. regional military weakness and failure to bring about a Middle Eastern peace settlement more than by Soviet subversion.

The crucial blows for the United States were the 1973 Middle East War, which precipitated OPEC's quadrupling oil prices, and the Iranian Revolution and the Iraqi-Iranian War, which caused a new rise in oil prices. The former arose from the determination of Sadat and Asad, disastrously underestimated in Jerusalem and Washington, to gain revenge and regain honor by attacking Israel, not from Soviet planning and execution. While Kissinger's turning toward Arab-Israeli even-handedness led to the Camp David agreements and thereby to at least the postponement of another Arab-Israeli War, this did not prevent the upward spiral of oil prices. The latest rise might have been avoided if Washington had realized early enough the danger to the Shah and influenced him toward earlier, more-gradual decompression. The Iranian Revolution destroyed U.S. influence in Iran and Iran's role as a regional force for stability in the Gulf and led to the Iraqi attack on Iran—all disasters for the United States. The 1981 crisis of the U.S. automobile industry, although primarily caused by its failure to anticipate higher gasoline prices, was in part the result of the fall of the Japanese yen subsequent to the post-revolutionary decline in Iranian oil production and the resultant greater competitiveness of Japanese automobiles in the U.S. market.[2] Then market forces and, secondarily, conservation and oil-price-produced recession began to take effect. By 1981, U.S. oil imports were down around 20 percent from the year before (from 8 to 6.5 million barrels per day), and there was a glut on the oil market, caused by higher oil prices, economic recession, and high Saudi oil production. Thus, OPEC price rises forced the U.S. consumer to help lower U.S. dependence on foreign oil and high Saudi production seemed likely to have at least temporarily stabilized oil prices.

Nevertheless, the oil-price shock, however relatively less it might become in the United States—and by mid-1981 the U.S. dollar had risen significantly vis-à-vis key West European currencies—had hurt the West German economy and was driving many Third World countries into near bankruptcy. And glut or not, economic stagnation, stagflation, rising unemployment, and prolonged low rates of growth remained the corroding products of the energy crisis.

Economics

Until 1973, Western Europe's and North America's economic problems had seemed containable. The main problem was inflation, resulting primarily from the U.S. deficit financing of the Vietnam War and the U.S. exportation of inflated dollars into the relatively uncontrollable Eurodollar market, and thereby the U.S. inflation went to Western Europe. West Germany, since 1945 the most fearful of, and therefore the most resistant to, inflation of any West European country, suffered from it the least; France and Italy more; and Great Britain, primarily due to its own decline, the most of all.

The first result was the international financial revolution of 1971—namely, Nixon's ending of the dollar's fixed convertibility into gold and the resultant floating of all major world currencies. While Nixon's move was the result of the economic recovery of Western Europe and Japan, which had made obsolete the post–World War II relationships of their currencies to the dollar, it was immediately caused by the inflationary impact of the Vietnam War and the resultant weakening of the dollar's position. The political result of this step was very difficult to gauge; one can only have impressions. Mine is that while floating brought OECD-currency relationships more in tune with economic-power relationships, and therefore in theory removed one strain from the Atlantic alliance, in fact it was such a blow to U.S. prestige, influence, and economic power that it contributed to weakening U.S. leadership in NATO.

The 1973 OPEC quadrupling of petroleum prices and the subsequent further price rises were much more-serious economic blows, particularly to some West European countries. For example, it intensified the stagflation characteristic of Italy and Great Britain. It greatly increased the balance-of-trade and balance-of-payments deficits of, and inflation in, many West European countries, primarily those that had no domestic sources of energy and that were also unable to increase their exports enough to balance the deficits caused by higher energy costs.

The net result was to increase the gap in Western Europe between West Germany plus those smaller countries associated with it in the European currency "snake" (Benelux, varying Scandinavian countries, and Austria) and the others—notably, Great Britain, France, and Italy. (In the OECD context Japan falls into the same category as West Germany.) Why did this gap occur? The explanation must begin with susceptibility to inflation. Those countries more caught up in inflation were, not surprisingly, those least able to cope with the quadrupling of energy costs; those least susceptible coped very well. West Germany was the best example of the latter because further inflation was initially avoided, and the balance of payments was kept positive, indeed improved, by two major policies—successful limiting of oil consumption and a successfully increased export drive to the OPEC countries, primarily Iran and the Arab oil-producing states. (Yet by late 1980 the oil price rises caused by the Iraqi-Iranian War hit even there; in 1981 West German growth was projected to be less than 1 percent, with resultant polarization in the SPD.) Even Italy suffered less than expected, also because of an intensified export drive. Nevertheless, to repeat, the net result was to increase the gap between West Germany and the countries associated with it in the currency snake and other West European countries. (It also resulted, because of slower West European growth, in greater Yugoslav and Romanian trade with the Comecon countries.)

In the late nineteenth century, the German economy had begun to outstrip the British. Later, the Japanese did the same. The two world wars in the short run interrupted, but in the long run accentuated, this process. The impact on the West European economies of the Vietnam War and the quadrupling of oil prices further sped up this trend.

The increasing economic gaps among the EEC countries made far more difficult the process of West European financial and monetary union (as a step toward political union). However, in 1978–1979 President Giscard d'Estaing and Chancellor Schmidt pushed through the European Monetary System (EMS). This was an enlarged and multilateralized snake, placing upper and lower limits on EEC currency fluctuations against each other, and thereby having them fluctuate more or less together against the dollar and the yen. The EMS was set up for four main reasons: (1) Giscard's desire to have international assistance and pressure to bring French inflation down; (2) Schmidt's desire to limit the upward revaluation of the deutsche mark in order to prevent German exports' being priced out of the market; (3) business pressure for stable currencies within the EEC; and (4) the lack of confidence of both countries in U.S. management of the dollar and their resultant determination to protect the EEC against its fall.

In the long range, it reflected the desire of both to regain momentum toward a West European confederation. Great Britain initially did not join the snake because of the pressure of Labour's left wing on the Callaghan government.

Moscow was against the snake because, despite its partial anti-U.S. overtones, the United States endorsed it, it tied France and Germany further together, increased West European power and cohesion, and demonstrated the lack of Soviet influence over such key West European developments.

The effect on the United States was more complex but finally negative as well. Higher energy costs, although important enough, were not the basic causes of U.S. economic problems. The key symptoms of the problems were decline of productivity and therefore of growth in per capita GNP, almost unique in the industrial world, but they had much deeper causes also: inadequate savings and investment; worker aversion to rapid technological change; too short-range corporate planning; and the outmoded governmental and economic systems, stymied by special-interest groups and harassed by antigrowth ideologies (opposition to massive nuclear and coal substitution for petroleum, priority for ecological considerations, "small is beautiful," and so forth). Was the United States faced, over and above the energy crisis, by British-type economic rot unless it rapidly and decisively changed its policies? It was too early to know, and in mid-1981 there were some indications to the contrary. For example, inflation was under ten percent; oil imports were down around 20 percent in 1980 from 1979; and the dollar was rising. Moreover, the historic passion for self-examination in the United States and its ruling conservatives' emphasis on deflation and growth would probably at least cut back, if not excise, the rot. Yet Japan was still likely to remain number one economically, and U.S. global power was seriously menaced by its domestic economic problems.

At first most West Europeans were convinced that the U.S. position had strengthened and that theirs had weakened because of the OPEC price rise. Western Europe (except, by the late 1970s, Norway and Great Britain) was far more dependent on OPEC oil than the United States, but it had little or no political influence in the Middle East, and the 1973 Middle East War, in which the United States and the USSR but not Western Europe played major roles, had triggered the oil embargo and, more important, the OPEC price rise.

After the OPEC price rise, the West European states, especially France, tried to improve relations with the Arab states, in part through the institutionalized Euro-Arab dialogue but primarily bilaterally. However, what the Arab states wanted—pressure on Israel, the highest levels of civil and military technology, and effective security relationships—the West Europeans could not give them, but the United States could and slowly, hesitantly, partially did. The United States also pushed through, over French opposition, the establishment of the International Energy Authority (IEA), which was supposed to coordinate the OECD countries' response to the energy crisis. However, it accomplished little except a contingency plan for sharing oil if another embargo and/or production cutback occurred—and one wonders how many of its members would carry it out in such a crisis.

Some French writers have maintained that the United States really triggered the energy crisis in order to recover the ground it lost from Vietnam and Watergate. No evidence exists for this, and indeed, as we shall soon see, U.S. financial suffering from it was only postponed. In part because of the energy crisis but also for cyclical reasons, especially the delayed international economic effect of U.S. deficit financing during the Vietnam War, the years immediately after the 1973 OPEC price quadrupling saw the most serious recession in the OECD countries since World War II. Because aggregate demand declined, the United States needed to import less oil. Moreover, this period was also one of worldwide grain shortages, notably in the USSR, so that the balance of payments was propped up by massive agricultural exports.

Second, by 1977 the U.S. balance of payments had turned massively negative. The economy was recovering faster than most of the West European ones, and thus its demand for energy increased. Despite the many warnings of an energy crisis and the efforts of the Ford and Carter administrations to limit petroleum consumption and develop petroleum substitutes, U.S. public apathy and special-interest lobbying in Congress long stalled any decisive action. Behind this apathy was a social and cultural lag. The U.S. public, accustomed to affluence and cheap energy and unaccustomed to dependence on foreign energy resources, did not, indeed probably soon could not, grasp the fact that its economic situation had fundamentally and, at least for the rest of this century, irreversibly changed. U.S. oil imports from abroad, and their cost, spiraled, and the U.S. balance-of-payments deficit thus spiraled upward. The consequences in 1978 were a precipitous decline of the dollar vis-à-vis the deutsche mark and the Swiss franc and, to a much lesser extent, vis-à-vis other OECD currencies and a further rise in U.S. inflation.[3]

Washington believed that the dollar's fall would so improve U.S. competitiveness that its balance-of-payments deficit would be largely corrected. However, the dollar's fall was so sharp that it fueled the already rising U.S. inflation by raising import prices and thereby domestic prices and threatened a stock market panic. Thus, in late 1978 the Carter administration took drastic measures to support the dollar and to give priority to fighting inflation rather than unemployment, whereupon the dollar recovered substantially, U.S. growth began to decline, and in early 1980 the U.S. economy moved into recession. However, the administration's attempts to meet the energy crisis were largely frustrated by Congress (which reflected public ignorance of the crisis), and the interruption of Iranian oil production in mid-1979 caused new major rises in oil prices and some temporary U.S. gasoline shortages, only relieved by a (temporary) Saudi increase in production. Although oil production soon again exceeded demand, U.S. inflation spiraled to 18 percent by early 1980, and the dollar so weakened that the administration felt compelled to introduce, under the leadership of Paul Volcker, the new chairman of the Federal Reserve Board, a classically deflation-ary program (of high interest rates and limited money supply). This triggered a recession, strengthened the dollar, and cut back inflation.

Soon, for a series of reasons, the United States ran a considerable current-account surplus. Moreover, the high interest rates so attracted foreign capital, and President Reagan's economic policies seemed so deflationary, that the dollar rose rapidly. Because of projected very low growth and fear of a Soviet invasion of Poland, the deutsche mark fell even more. West Germany was compelled to raise its interest rates in order to cut back capital flight to the United States, and thus pay more for its dollar-denominated oil imports and run the risk of a reces-sion. Chancellor Schmidt publicly criticized Washington for this. This episode demonstrated the interdependence of the OECD economies and the political tensions that could arise from their being out of phase. It also showed that Western Europe resented U.S. deflation (through high interest rates) almost as much as inflation because both made management of its own economies much more difficult. Economic interdependence had come with a vengeance.

Thus, by mid-1981, the United States and the other principal industrial countries, except West Germany and Japan, were still in the grip of stagflation— that is, prolonged low growth, high inflation, and unemployment due to loss of governments' political ability to keep down the growth in money supply and the resultant antigrowth volatility of financial markets. It seemed likely that stagflation could only be overcome by such a drastic deflationary shock that the built-in psychological expectations of inflation by the business and financial community would be destroyed and investment confidence and growth thereby restored, as it was in West Germany after the 1948 currency reform. Such a shock would only be possible if governments would give it overriding priority vis-à-vis keeping down unemployment and interest rates. For welfare capitalist states this was politically extremely difficult, since it would mean an economic counterrevolution against the so-called revolution of social welfare entitlements. However, until this was done, stagflation and low growth seemed likely to con-tinue. Mrs. Thatcher was not keeping down public expenditures and money supply increase, and she seemed unlikely to find it politically possible to do so enough to break out of the British stagflation.[4] Whether President Reagan could manage politically to do so, as he was trying, remained to be seen.

Eastern Europe

The economic problems of Eastern Europe in the late 1970s had structural and energy aspects.[5] The former were similar to those of the more-developed parts of the USSR. By the late 1970s, most of Eastern Europe was, or was rapidly becoming, economically developed. Its main structural problem, therefore, was the increasing irrelevance of the Stalinist centralized model to a developed economy. Decentralization, increased financial incentives, and a more rational price system were imperative if technological progress was to come anywhere close to the technological leap forward of the OECD countries. The same was true for agriculture because collective farms are never productive. Such measures were rather successfully introduced into Yugoslavia after 1951. Yet they limit the control of technologically less-competent Communist party officials over the economy and have been only slowly and very partially introduced in Eastern Europe. Therefore, East European–manufactured goods, made with lower-level technology and much less worker productivity than those in the West, have not been competitive in the world market.

In order to increase productivity, and also to decrease political dissent, especially among workers, most East European states in the 1960s and 1970s introduced some limited, modified consumerism—that is, they tried to satisfy consumer demand by producing, and especially by importing, more consumer goods. Gierek also unsuccessfully tried to make Polish industry productive and exports competitive by massive foreign credits. But, as the French say, the appetite grows with eating. This proved to be the case in Poland in 1970, 1976, and most seriously in 1980.

The other East European economies were not much better. None of them was in such a crisis, with such political repercussions, as Poland's, but they all lagged behind their goals for the structural reasons set forth in the previous discussion. Hungary's economic reforms, initially so promising, had been cut back, although not so much as East Germany's. In sum, East European economic problems continued and in some respects intensified.

The USSR and Eastern Europe had expected that détente would bring them large inputs of Western credits and technology. This turned out to be true from Western Europe, notably from West Germany (as a part of *Ostpolitik*), France, and Italy. Initial Eastern hopes that the United States would become deeply involved in such transfers were frustrated by the impact in the United States of Soviet and East European dissidence. The Jackson-Vanik and Stevenson amendments greatly limited any credits that the USSR could get to finance trade with the United States. The greater debt-service payments would probably make Comecon look more inward and import fewer Western goods. The East had either to export salable goods to the West or reschedule the debts. In the case of Poland, whose Western debts by early 1981 were over $25 billion, and yearly repayments of principal and interest $7 billion, rescheduling became unavoidable.

The dream of some people in the West—that the East would become so dependent on Western high-level technology as to restrain Eastern behavior—proved illusory. The Jackson-Vanik amendment, on the one hand, probably prevented the East from being as restrained as it might otherwise have been. On the other hand, the East was less able to improve its technology (including military technology) than had been expected and than the West had feared.

The malaise that affected Soviet-U.S. détente led the United States to increase technology transfer to China. In 1977, the U.S. Department of Commerce refused to license the shipment of a large computer to the USSR but permitted the sale of two smaller computers to China. This move made the Soviets more suspicious but hardly put enough pressure on them to compensate for it. In 1979–1981, especially after the Soviet invasion of Afghanistan, U.S. economic relations with China improved even more, some U.S. sales were licensed that could be of military value to the Chinese, and the Reagan administration decided to sell some weapons to Beijing.

The energy crisis intensified the economic problems of Eastern Europe. Before it, their economic relations with the USSR had been in at least one respect becoming more advantageous for the USSR shipped to Eastern Europe more and cheaper raw materials than Eastern Europe shipped manufactured goods to the USSR. The USSR, however, which politically and militarily dominated Eastern Europe, was naturally unwilling to let itself thus be economically colonized by its own political colonies. Moscow tried to meet this problem in two ways: It increased Comecon integration so that it could handle this problem more centrally and efficiently, and it got the East European states to invest in Soviet raw-material production.

Enter the 1973 energy crisis. It may seem, and indeed did so seem to many in the West, that the USSR, and Comecon as a whole, benefited from it vis-à-vis the West because the USSR was an oil-exporting country, while Eastern and Western Europe were not and the United States was ceasing to be. However, the energy crisis also greatly accentuated the differences in economic interests between Moscow and Eastern Europe. As an oil exporter, the USSR wanted to profit from higher oil prices to raise its own oil-export prices to Eastern Europe, while the oil-importing East European states wanted to buy their oil as cheaply as possible. The Soviets initially declared that they would not allow this to influence intra-Comecon solidarity, and indeed they raised their own oil prices considerably more slowly than OPEC did to the West. Moreover, some East European states were already importing oil from OPEC countries, and the USSR might well have to in the late 1980s as well. (Moscow had reportedly already informed the East European states that they would not be able to rely on Soviet oil imports so much in the future.) Thus, the net oil price rise in Eastern Europe, even if delayed, would eventually be almost if not as substantial as in Western Europe.

How can the East Europeans pay for their rising oil costs? They can hardly do it from their own strained resources. They must therefore either export more in the world market or be subsidized by Soviet loans or aid. Reluctant to accept the latter, Moscow was moving toward the former. However, the former required major inputs of Western technology into Eastern Europe, significant reform of its economic system, and increasing interdependence with the world economy, particularly with Western Europe, all policies which Moscow had so far deemed contrary to its economic and political interests.

Most East Europeans states seemed therefore likely to become more financially dependent upon the USSR. (Poland and Romania, because of their coal and oil resources respectively, could be partial exceptions.) Moscow could therefore exercise more political pressure on the East European states, but the East European populations would become increasingly resentful of this pressure, as they would of rising energy prices and importation of Western inflation.

Thus the Soviet position in Eastern Europe was not improved by the energy crisis, although its energy-exporting position certainly was. The Soviets would have gained much more if one of their initial major hopes from détente—massive Western and Japanese investments in the extraction of oil and natural gas from Siberia—had materialized, but it had not and seemed less likely than ever to do so.

However, although the Soviets have gained and will continue to in Eastern Europe, and vis-à-vis the OECD countries, in economic strength as a result of the energy crisis, they have suffered political losses elsewhere, notably in the Middle East. The enormously increased dollar revenues that OPEC brought to Iran, Libya, and Algeria decreased those countries' financial and therefore political dependence on the USSR for they now pay hard currency for Soviet arms. They shifted considerably from (inferior) Soviet to (superior) Western technology. Saudi Arabia's much larger oil revenues enabled it to become the paymaster of much of the Middle East on an anti-Soviet and anticommunist platform. While the Arab regrouping caused by the Egyptian-Israeli peace treaty decreased U.S. influence in Saudi Arabia, Jordan, and other traditionalist Arab states, and the Iranian Revolution wrecked it in Iran, neither development increased Soviet influence there. On the contrary, the regrouping made Iraq move away from Moscow toward Saudi Arabia and thereby further diminished Soviet influence in Baghdad.

One other problem had cast its shadows before. Projections of future OECD oil consumption and probable new oil discoveries differed greatly. Some observers felt that consumption of oil would rise so rapidly and that new discoveries would be so insufficient to cover it that in the mid-1980s only a major increase in production by Saudi Arabia, the only oil producer with sufficient reserves, could prevent a major, long-term, global shortage. The shortage as such will not actually materialize, for its global anticipation will produce a rise in oil prices, over and above whatever OPEC may otherwise do, sufficient to reduce oil consumption to correspond to supply. If it did occur, such a rise in oil prices would produce major economic dislocations in the OECD countries and, to a lesser extent, the East European countries as well and perhaps even in the USSR. The oil shortage and OPEC price rises showed that such a prospect could occur. Yet by mid-1981, due to higher prices and Western conservation, there was in fact at least a temporary oil glut. Thus, the market mechanism described previously was already in operation.

4

Dissidence in the USSR and Eastern Europe

This chapter analyzes the effect of dissidence upon Soviet-U.S. relations in general and in Europe in particular. The effect may be direct: the USSR and the East European states have often seen the extent and seriousness of the dissidence as so great that they feel compelled to increase their repressive measures, or it may be indirect: the extent and seriousness of the dissidence, and repression of it, may decrease Western support and increase active opposition to détente.

Dissidence in the USSR after Stalin

Stalin's reign of terror was so great and society and political activity therefore so atomized that dissidents did not then dare raise their heads.[1] Khrushchev tried that most difficult of all political arts—controlled decompression—which he believed would increase economic growth and revitalize Communist ideology. He came to think, however, and his successor Brezhnev even more so, that he had gone too far, and repression increased again, although not up to Stalin's level. Khrushchev's thaw produced a remarkable flowering of political, intellectual, ethnic, and religious dissidence. It was encouraged by the Soviet elite's knowledge of Stalin's crimes, by the example, as so frequently in Soviet history, of a few noble, heroic figures, of which the most famous have been Aleksandr Solzhenitsyn and Andrei Sakharov, and by East-West détente itself, which raised dissidents' hopes and for a time limited police repression against them.

Soviet dissidence has been more ethical and moral than political because major political change seemed so unlikely and mass support for dissidence so lacking. Its ideas have reflected almost the full gamut of pre-Bolshevik Russia; indeed, it has revived all the currents of the political culture of the Russian Empire. Although it has in part been Westernizing in accord with the Russian tradition of support for the West European model of modernization and democratization, the other Russian tradition, the populist one represented notably by Solzhenitsyn, has also been prominent, has had more mass support, and is intensifying. Although initially the "true Leninists" seemed also significant—for example, the brothers Medvedev—their weakness soon became apparent. Indeed, they themselves, while posing as true Leninists, were in fact largely social democrats. If they had not been at first, one would have expected that they would become so rapidly.

The main reason why the populist dissidents have enjoyed more public sympathy than the Westernizers or the true Leninists has been, of course, Great Russian nationalism. The USSR is also the Russian Empire—that is, the rule by the Great Russians (now only around half the Soviet population) over the other nations of the USSR. (In a more-indirect sense, they rule most of Eastern Europe as well.) In all likelihood, the vast majority of Great Russians find this not only desirable but essential. (After all, Pushkin bitterly denounced the Western critics of the tsar's suppression of the Polish rising of 1830, including his great friend Mickiewicz, and Herzen's support of the Polish rising of 1863 ruined his political influence in Russia.) Were the non-Great Russian nations of the USSR to be free to secede, or even to obtain genuine autonomy, the USSR might well no longer remain a superpower. At least its power would be greatly diminished by nationalist strife.

Most of the Westernizing, true Leninists and, uniquely, one of the populist dissidents, Solzhenitsyn, favor self-determination for the non–Great Russian Soviet nations. This alone prevents them from obtaining mass Great Russian support. There is another reason why they cannot obtain it in the foreseeable future—namely, the historic passivity of the Great Russian masses and the great majority of the Great Russian intelligentsia. Historically, Russia's rulers have regarded it as their patrimony—that is, they think, and so do their subjects, that they *own* the land and people. Moreover, they were always even more ambivalent than those they ruled toward the West. They wanted its technology but feared its liberal and democratic ideas. Indeed, one fruitful way to study Russian history is to study the tension produced by their attempts to get the former but not the latter. Modern Russian dissidence was limited, violence oriented, and conspiratorial. It sparked such repression by the tsars, notably by Alexander III after the assassination of his father Alexander II by the minuscule terrorist Narodnaya Volya, that Imperial Russia became a vast police state.

The tsarist regime did not collapse of its own accord and certainly not because of its dissidents. It fell because it was defeated in war, first in the Russo-Japanese War of 1905 and then, catastrophically, in World War I. Had this not occurred, and despite the stupidity and incompetence of the last tsar, Nicholas II, Lenin would have remained an unknown exile and most of the Russian Left would probably have become increasingly involved in the continuation of the remarkably successful pre-1914 modernization of the Russian Empire.

By 1914, indeed by 1905, however, Russia was militarily much weaker than its then main enemies, Germany and Japan. Since atomic weapons did not exist, war seemed still a rational instrument of politics. But now the situation is reversed. The USSR is exceeded only by the United States in military power. Nuclear weapons have frozen boundaries where nuclear weapons face each other directly. Thus, Soviet military defeat is no longer likely. Dissidence in the USSR, therefore, seems condemned to political impotence.

This is so despite the fact that dissidence among the non–Great Russian nations of the USSR has been more intense and extensive than among the Great Russians; nor is this surprising. While Great Russian nationalism works against liberal dissidence in the USSR, the nationalisms of the other nations within the USSR, and a fortiori of these East European nations outside it but controlled by it, are on the side of the dissidents. This is particularly true if the dissidents are in an area of the USSR that was not a part of it before 1939 and/or in which religion interacts with nationalism as in Poland (for example, Catholicism in Lithuania and, perhaps in the future, Islam in Soviet Central Asia) and is a nation that has traditionally been a part of, or strongly influenced by, Western or Central Europe (for example, the western Ukraine or the Baltic states.) When the non–Great Russian nations were conquered and, to a greater or lesser extent, colonized by the Great Russians, many of them, including Georgia and Armenia, were—what is more important, thought they were—at a higher level of cultural development, and in some cases, of economic development as well, than the Great Russians. This was the reverse of the situation of the French when they conquered their African colonies. The conquering Russian imperial power was seen by many of the nations it conquered to be superior only in military power but inferior in most or all other respects.

One Soviet group, a mixture of nation and religious and ethnic group, the Jews, needs special attention because of its importance in Soviet dissidence and its great impact in the West. Historically, primarily because of tsarist persecution and discrimination against them, most politically active Jews in the Russian Empire either emigrated, most to the United States and only a minority to Palestine; remained relatively passive; joined the Soviet radical-Marxist movements, the Bolsheviks and the Mensheviks; or became assimilated (for example, Pasternak's conversion to Russian Orthodoxy.) Stalinist antisemitism, limited but still continued by his successors, drove some of those who remained into dissidence. (Others like the writer Ehrenburg always remained loyal to the regime.)

Thus, two major motives existed for Jewish dissidence. The first was that some Jews who consciously remained apart from the USSR's history and culture were dissidents like their non-Jewish Great Russian comrades. Indeed, they provided a large percentage, although not a majority, of Russian-speaking dissidents. Second, others became Zionists, primarily out of despair that they could never avoid discrimination in the USSR and/or because they were emotionally transformed by the Israeli victories in the 1967 Middle East War and because the end of mass police terror and their increasing knowledge about Israel mobilized them politically, and sometimes also religiously, toward Zionism.

We cannot know how many Soviet Jews (of the approximately two million) would, if they felt they had a free choice, become dissidents, Zionist or not. If only because of the repression, only a small minority have done so; the majority, like the other Soviet nations, has remained passive, and another minority has actively supported the ruling party. However, as Soviet repression of dissidence increased, repression vis-à-vis Jews was, paradoxically, both more and less than that vis-à-vis other nations.

More, because the Soviets since Stalin have been "pragmatically" antisemitic—that is, Khrushchev and his successors wanted to remove Jews from leading positions because they thought them an unnecessary source of popular hostility to their rule. Moreover, the Israeli successes in the 1967 war, increasing Soviet support for the most radical and anti-Israeli Arabs, and Jewish-dissident activism made official Soviet antisemitism increase further.

The Soviets were also less repressive toward some of the Soviet Jews because Western, particularly U.S., pressure was strong on their behalf. Moscow was therefore more inclined to let them emigrate, to Israel. However, most dissident Soviet Jews were not Zionists and emigrated directly or via Israel to the United States or Western Europe. By thus exporting dissident Soviet Jews, Moscow placated Western outrage and rid itself of the leaders of the Zionist dissident movement and many leaders in other dissident groups as well.

Soviet Dissidence and the West

The influence of Soviet dissidence in the West has been much greater than in the USSR. Especially in the United States, it eroded support of détente. It also helped estrange some leading Western European Communist parties from Moscow.

To understand the West's perceptions and misperceptions of the Soviet dissident movement, we much consider the historical and psychological background as well as its immediate impact. The West was preconditioned by its knowledge, and often memories, of tsarist oppression and antitsarist opposition to expect that Soviet dissidence would exist and, as Lenin showed, could be successful. Khrushchev's revelation of Stalin's crimes made Soviet dissidence morally even more noble. That the dissidents' motives were primarily ethical and moral, not political, also strengthened their appeal. The world-famous persecution and heroism of Solzhenitsyn and Sakharov, the millions of copies of Solzhenitsyn's writings, and the continuing heroic struggle of Sakharov and the support for him by Western scientists did the same. The Moscow dissidents skillfully used Western correspondents in Moscow and, through them, Western radio stations broadcasting to the USSR and Western communications media. They thus enhanced their reputation and spread their ideas throughout much of the Soviet intelligentsia (although few followed their example) and in the West. Those who fled or, like Solzhenitsyn, were driven abroad continued to denounce the soviet regime with considerable effect. Solzhenitsyn's greatest achievement in the West was to discredit the Soviet system by his *Gulag Archipelago,* which overshadowed his anti-Westernizing, Slavophil, antidemocratic political philosophy. The social-democratic ideas of the Westernizers appealed much more to the West European and U.S. Left.

The dissidents' effect in the West was an important impetus, but only an intensifying one in the postwar discrediting in Western Europe of the USSR as a model. (It had been discredited in the United States after 1948.) Moscow's suppression of the 1956 Hungarian Revolution had been a blow to Soviet prestige in the European Left, but the anti-Americanism produced by the Vietnam War overshadowed it. In 1968, the West's enthusiasm for the Czechoslovak reform wave was so great that the Soviet invasion of Czechoslovakia was a near death blow to what remained of Soviet influence in the West European Left. The initial prestige won for Moscow by the Soviet sputnik was also overshadowed by Western technological progress, notably by U.S. superiority in space. The end of the Vietnam War removed the main source of European anti-Americanism. The Sino-Soviet split and the West European communist condemnation of the Soviet invasion of Czechoslovakia destroyed any belief in Western Europe in the Soviet version of proletarian internationalism.

Finally, Western revulsion against Soviet suppression of its dissidents merged into the human-rights movement. (Western outrage against the suppression of dissidence in post-Allende Chile, the Shah's Iran, and Amin's Uganda did as well.) The global activity of Amnesty International also played a significant role as did President Carter's espousal of the human-rights cause. Indeed, the main reason why human rights became such a popular cause, particularly in the United States, was that it was one of the few issues on which Right and Left could unite.

By mid-1981, the Great Russian dissident movement seemed to have been largely broken up. (This had not occurred to such an extent, for example, in Lithuania, which has the same combination of nationalism and Roman Catholicism as Poland.) Solzhenitsyn was in Vermont, Sakharov was in exile in Gorky, and a significant part of the Soviet intelligentsia was in New York, Paris, and Israel.

Yet caution is in order. All dissident movements throughout Russian history have failed politically, with the exceptions of the February and October Revolutions, and they occurred only because the USSR had been defeated by Japan and Imperial Germany respectively. However, dissidence has always reemerged. Dissidents have usually wanted to set a moral example and have at least succeeded in that. Given Russian history, could more have been, or be, expected?[2]

Eastern Europe

Dissidence has been quite different in Eastern Europe, particularly in Poland, East Germany, and Czechoslovakia, because East European nationalism intensifies it.[3] East European traditions have primarily been influenced by Western Europe. Social democratic and Catholic ideologies remain far stronger than Leninism. The East European peoples are more politically active, and police repression is less than in the USSR. The inflow of Western ideas, technology, and mass culture is much greater. For most East Europeans, the USSR is backward and therefore all the less their legitimate hegemonic power. West European Marxism, including the West European Communist parties, has been more influential in Eastern Europe than in the USSR, as has the impact of the CSCE Final Act and Carter's human-rights policy. The great attraction of Western, particularly U.S. and West German, technology further discredited the Soviet model of economics and technology. The demonstration effect of Western Europe increased the more détente facilitated travel, notably of West Germans to East Germany. In order to raise their economic growth rate and pay for the higher-priced Soviet oil they import, the East Europeans tried to improve the technological level of their export goods so they would sell in Western markets. Because they largely failed to accomplish this, the Soviet industrial model was further discredited.

Eastern Europe is a nonregion: East Germany is Central Europe, and Albania is almost Middle Eastern. The East European dissident movements were therefore very different in origin and nature, and they had different effects on different countries in the West. Sociologically, they have reflected the reassertion of the traditional East European authority of the intelligentsia and especially of creative intellectuals.

Dissidence in East European countries has varied not only in origins but also in length and intensity. Before 1956 in Hungary and 1968 in Czechslovakia, it centered among communist intellectuals and activists, spread to nonparty creative intellectuals, then to students and the mass-communication media, and only at the end to workers. (Peasants were little affected.)

These culturally preindustrial movements were like the intelligentsia-based Polish rebellions and the Hungarian rising in the nineteenth century. They were crushed in Plzeň and East Berlin in 1953, in Budapest in 1956, and in Prague in 1968—by the communist regimes and the Red Army. (Such movements never occurred in Romania, Bulgaria, and Albania.) What has been their legacy?

In Hungary, Kádár, head of Hungary's Communist party, instituted a new *Ausgleich,* like Ferenc Deák after 1867, this time with Moscow instead of Vienna—the greatest example of the self-rehabilitation of a quisling in modern history. Hungarian cultural life after 1956 has been effectively controlled, especially to prevent any published criticism of the USSR. Yet Kádár's policies have not only been consumerist. Rather, the shock of the defeat of the Hungarian Revolution, relative economic prosperity, and the potential threat of Soviet if not Hungarian repression have led to a consensus for national self-restraint. Thus, overt Hungarian dissidence has been small indeed and those few who tried to defy the regime, such as the small group that had formed around the great Marxist philosopher Lukács, were allowed to emigrate.

1981 was nearly thirteen years after the Soviet invasion of Czechoslovakia. Thirteen years after the Soviet invasion of Hungary in 1956 the *Ausgleich* had already occurred. However, post-1968 Czechoslovakia has remained a desert that only communists call peace. The historical political caution of the Czechs and Slovaks precluded any mass-dissident movement. Although repression was extensive, a small, intellectual dissident movement, "Charter 77," survived despite the forcing into exile of many of its leaders. Its political views were those of Masaryk, the philosopher, and social democracy more than true Leninism. Like Soviet dissidence, its effect was greater in the West than in Czechoslovakia, but it did show there also that Husák and his colleages are quislings indeed. Why does such a desert of peace still cover Czechoslovakia? Perhaps because its democratic tradition in Czechoslovakia is too strong. Perhaps also because, alas, Husák is not Kádár.

The East European country where dissent has had the most effect on any Western country is the one in which, until 1976, dissidence seemed hardly to exist—East Germany. But much has happened there since: the deprivation of citizenship of the balladeer Wolf Biermann; the house arrest of the longtime dissident Robert Havemann; the petition of most of East Germany's top literary figures in favor of Biermann; the revisionist book published in West Germany by Rudolf Bahro and his subsequent imprisonment; the late 1977 (probably genuine) "Manifesto" by revisionist communists within the SED that showed the great influence of West European communism and strong advocacy of a reunited, neutral Germany; and the regime pressure that forced a significant number of writers to emigrate to West Germany. Up to 100,000 East Germans reportedly applied for legal permission to go there as well.

Behind all this has been the effect of West German *Ostpolitik*. It resulted in yearly visits to East Germany by six million West Germans; the regular watching of West German television by 80 percent of the East German population (the rest cannot receive it); and the impact in East Germany of the CSCE Final Act and, particularly within the ruling SED, of the ideas of such West European communist leaders as Carrillo.

These East German developments have had considerable impact in West Germany. Dissidence in East Germany proves to many West Germans, especially the liberal and leftist intelligentsia, that East Germans have not resigned themselves to Soviet hegemony, authoritarian rule, and the division of Germany and that the substance of the German nation, whose preservation has been *Ostpolitik*'s chief objective, is indeed being preserved.

Yugoslavia played a positive role in détente and may, if things go badly there, play a negative one in the future. Ever since the 1948 Soviet-Yugoslav break, Yugoslavia profited from Soviet-U.S. conflict and wanted Soviet-U.S. détente because of the break—that is, it has been able to play one superpower off against the other and thus profit from their competition. Tito's rapprochment with China further increased his ability to do so. Yugoslavia wants détente because it fears that it would be inevitably involved in a superpower military conflict and because it believes that détente makes it less likely that the USSR would use or threaten to use military force against it.

Dissidence in Yugoslavia, as before World War II, has tended to be ethnically polarized, notably in Croatia and largely Albanian Kosovo, where dissidence combines nationalist and liberal motives. The events of 1971 in Croatia, when Tito suppressed a massive student- and intellectual-based dissident movement, combining the drives for Croatian nationalist assertion and liberations, showed how susceptible Yugoslavia was, and how much more it would be after Tito, to nationalistically based dissident movements. (The Western Marxist-oriented group of philosophers around the formerly published magazine *Praxis* has little mass base and is hardly a threat to regime control.) The bloody 1981 Albanian nationalist riots in Kosovo where Albanian irredentism clashed with Serb chauvinism also illustrated its susceptibility. Moreover, there have been enough signs of Soviet fishing in these troubled waters for the Yugoslavs and the West to be concerned about the dangers to post-Tito Yugoslav independence and therefore to East-West détente. Although I would not expect Yugoslavia to break apart and initially there was a post-Tito demonstration of national unity, national tensions combined perhaps with liberalizing tendencies are likely to reassert themselves in Croatia, as they already have in Kosovo, and Serb chauvinism in reaction to them. Thus in mid-1981 nationalist dissent in Yugoslavia boded ill for the stability of the state.

5 The USSR, The United States, and the West European Left

A few years ago, when the Italian communists seemed likely to enter governments in Rome, many Western observers feared that Soviet influence in Western Europe would therefore grow. In 1981, in contrast, communist participation in Italian government seemed much less likely. The relations between the Soviet and the Italian and Spanish Communist parties were worse than ever before. The West European Socialist parties were on even worse terms with Moscow.[1] Soviet attractiveness and prestige in West European leftist intellectual circles had largely collapsed. Soviet attractiveness to West Europeans, in contrast to the fear its military power aroused in them, was thus at a new low.

Eurocommunism and the CPSU

The neologism *Eurocommunism* is less accurate now than it was in the 1970s when it seemed for a time that not only the Italian (PCI) and Spanish (PCE) but also the French Communist party (PCF) were moving toward much the same mixture of reformism and nationalism that had characterized the Social Democratic party in Imperial Germany and, to a lesser extent, Yugoslav communism after 1951. The PCI and PCE turned to reformism, a blurred area between Leninism and social democracy, because revolution had failed and electoral gains required it. They also turned to nationalism for the same reason and because the PCI and PCE leaderships, and to a lesser extent their followers, had become disillusioned with the USSR and its hegemonic policies toward them and were attracted to a semialigned European regionalism. Thus, Eurocomminusm in Italy and Spain, as in Hungary, Czechoslovakia, and Poland, was a revival of the traditional political culture of the European Left.

Eurocommunism replaced the leading role of the Soviet Communist Party (CPSU) in the international communist movement with the assertion of each party's autonomy. It exchanged alliance with the CPSU for one with the Yugoslav and Romanian parties. It exchanged the universal applicability of the Bolshevik Revolution and the Soviet model of real socialism—violent revolution and the "dictatorship of the proletariat" (that is, of the Communist party) for reform of Leninism and Marxism to fit each country's history, traditions, and political culture. In sum, it became both nationalist and internationalist (not Soviet dominated). Such reformism, the Eurocommunists held, has to be different in highly industrialized societies such as Western Europe from Lenin's semideveloped Russia—indeed, a "third way." (The Japanese and Australian Communist parties, not surprisingly, have followed similar paths as, in Latin America, have the Venezuelan MAS and the Brazilian Communist party.[2]) This third way included working-class pluralism, not the leading role of the Communist party; the shared interest of mankind to avoid nuclear war and therefore in détente and an ambivalent, not totally hostile, attitude toward NATO; and to a greater or lesser degree, the guarantee, including after socialism triumphed, of civil liberties, a multiparty system, and the reversibility of socialism—in sum, the move from proletarian to "new" internationalism through democratic nationalism. Yet democratic centralism, the historical inevitability of socialism, antiimperialism, and party relations with the CPSU remained. Eurocommunism still is not, nor is it likely soon to become, social democracy.

Eurocommunist reformism threatened Soviet policies in Western Europe, the USSR, and Eastern Europe, and those toward China as well because it refused to learn from, defend, and praise the USSR and the so-called general laws of real socialism that Moscow claims it primarily exemplifies. Compared to these heresies, Eurocommunist support of most of Soviet foreign policy, especially aid to national liberation movements, and opposition to capitalism and "Atlanticism" (that is, U.S. influence and presence in Western Europe), while welcome, was less important to Moscow.

Until 1978, Moscow thus saw Eurocommunism as a serious problem. However, in September 1977 the PCF backed out of its coalition with the socialists, and for that reason Giscard won the presidential election. Thereupon the PCF abandoned most of its reformism and autonomy from the CPSU, reverted to its traditional Jacobin-nationalist posture, and supported the Soviet invasion of Afghanistan. The CPSU since has had no significant problems with the PCF but it has continued to feud with the PCI and PCE. Ironically, Mitterand's mid-1981 landslide victory marked both a historic defeat for the PCF, their worst one in post-1944 French history, and the entry of four PCF ministers, in minor posts, into the new French government. Whether the PCF would be imprisoned by, or profit from, this defeat cloaked in victory remained to be seen. In any case, the absolute socialist majority in the new French parliament at least temporarily destroyed the PCF's claim to be the representative of the French working class as well as ended decades of right-wing rule in France. Given Mitterand's continued criticism of Soviet policy and his support of LRTNF deployment, it may well turn out to have been a defeat for Moscow as well.

The PCI and PCE have also recently been politically unsuccessful. The PCI's *compromesso storico* (that is, entry into the government as a minority partner with the Christian Democrats) collapsed in 1979 after the Christian Democrats accepted the PCI's parliamentary support but rejected its entry into the government. Thereafter the PCI lost votes, and the socialists gained. By early 1981, the PCI leadership had abandoned the *compromesso storico,* at least as long as the present Christian Democratic leadership was in power. The PCI lost votes because its traditionalist members felt that it had cooperated too much with the Christian Democrats, and its reformist members became convinced that the government it had supported but not joined was more incompetent than before. Moreover, the PCI electoral losses were primarily in southern Italy, which felt that it had not profited enough from the PCI's support of the government.[3] However, although the CPSU may have hoped that the PCI losses would make it less reformist, the contrary occurred. In early 1981, the PCI leadership committed itself to the kind of discussion of draft policy positions that Leninist democratic centralism would have excluded.

The PCE remained a minor factor in Spanish political life. The Spanish Socialist party, the only credible alternative governmental party, refused to ally with the PCE, and in early 1981 in Catalonia, the regionally autonomist Catalonist Communist party, briefly and to Soviet applause, rejected Eurocommunism.[4]

For Moscow this was only part of the problem. The challenge by Eurocommunism to Soviet legitimacy at home and abroad, to its hegemony in Eastern Europe, and to its struggle with Beijing had become more serious because of the developments in Poland and the resumption of party relations between the Chinese and the PCI and PCE. Soviet problems with the Eurocommunist parties are thus those of devolution of empire.

The CPSU is a party that controls, and therefore is usually primarily interested in, a state, while the Eurocommunist parties want to but do not have state power. Moreover, the CPSU has been until recently a globally hegemonic party, and it is still regionally hegemonic in most of Eastern Europe and among the small Communist parties of the Middle East and Latin America. The CPSU is a declining imperial party, however, while the USSR is a rising imperial power. Because the Eurocommunist parties have so closely allied with the Yugoslav and Romanian parties, Soviet policy toward one must be closely interrelated with its policy toward the other.

Since Suslov, the chief Soviet ideologist, first proclaimed them after the Hungarian Revolution, Moscow has been propagating its general laws of real socialism: the leading role of the Communist party, nationalization of all the means of production, and proletarian internationalism that is in fact, although not in theory, the leading role of the CPSU.

Yet Moscow compromised with the PCI and PCE. However, it never compromised on its condemnation of anti-Sovietism (that is, ideological rejection of real socialism) or on the leading role of the Communist party once real socialism triumphed. Soviet views on these have differed only tactically, particularly when targets of opportunity presented themselves such as the prospect, in the mid-1970s, that the pro-Soviet Portuguese Communist party might take, or participate in, power.

Later, when Soviet policy hardened toward China and the United States, polemics with the PCI and the PCE intensified. In 1980, the PCI and PCE, to

Moscow's fury, resumed party relations with the Chinese Communist party (CCP);[5] the ex-Eurocommunist PCF returned to the Soviet camp;[6] and the remaining Eurocommunists boycotted the April 1980 Soviet-sponsored European Communist conference in Paris.

The resumption of PCI-CCP relations had been a long time coming. Berlinguer had unsuccessfully tried it in 1971 and presumably several times thereafter. Moscow's opposition slowed down his efforts. However, his principal obstacle was that Beijing wanted the PCI to become anti-Soviet. Because in the 1960s Mao had denounced Togliatti and the PCI as more revisionist than the CPSU, his death was probably also a precondition for resumption of PCI-CCP relations. Finally, Deng Xiaoping's victory over the "Gang of Four" led to domestic reformism and pragmatic rapprochement with the United States within the context of Chinese priority for encirclement of the USSR. Thus the policy differences the PCI and the CCP had had before Mao's death had been largely eroded by revisionism in China's policies and by the hardening of Moscow's line.

Berlinguer visited China 14–23 April 1980. He got the resumption of CCP-PCI relations on the basis of their agreement to disagree about the CPSU. Beijing probably felt that even this contributed to encirclement of the USSR, while the PCI became communist neutralist between the CPSU and the CCP, the logical consequence of the Eurocommunist autonomist position and one that Romania had drawn much earlier.

That same year Berlinguer had long, cordial conversations at the European parliament at Strasbourg with François Mitterand, the head of the French Socialist party, and Willy Brandt, the chairman of the SPD and the Socialist International. He was reacting to Marchais's trip to Moscow, his endorsement of the Soviet invasion of Afghanistan, and his near total realignment with Soviet policies, and to the invitation by French and Polish Communist parties, at Soviet prompting, to the other European Communist parties to attend a conference in Paris—one that Berlinguer had presumably already decided to boycott.

The PCF's return to Moscow cemented the PCI-PCE reformist axis in Western Europe and the pan-European PCI-PCE-Yugoslav-Romanian autonomist axis. They all refused to attend the Paris conference, which endorsed the Soviet line.

Thus, the CPSU repudiated the concessions that had made the 1976 East Berlin conference possible and its attendance and results unanimous. Moscow did so because détente had given way to a new cold war in the Third World, the Soviet Union was nearly isolated on the Afghanistan issue, and it consequently preferred to have fewer but more-reliable communist supporters of its foreign policies. Moscow thus decided to abandon, at least temporarily, its attempt to gain support from the Eurocommunists (and the Yugoslavs and Romanians) in favor of Lenin's policy, "Better fewer but better." Moscow therefore staged European communist conferences only with its supporters and attacked the PCI's "new internationalism." Yet Moscow's desire to divide Western Europe from the United States on arms control and Third-World issues made a Soviet break with the Eurocommunists the more unlikely. Whether the CPSU will soon, or ever, again compromise with this Eurocommunist autonomist axis remains to be seen. As of mid-1981, the relations between the CPSU and it were very strained, its international ties more diverse, and the prospects for European (and international) Communist unity never less.

Nevertheless, unless the USSR invaded Poland, the Eurocommunists did not want to break off party relations with the CPSU for reasons of common historical identity and ideology (with the Bolshevik Revolution, not with Soviet real socialism); because they believed it contrary to their ideology since it would antagonize both the pro-Soviet and working class elements in their base; and because it would limit their access to, and influence in, Eastern Europe and the USSR itself. Conversely, contrary to its previous practice—for example, with Tito—the CPSU had not broken off party relations with the Eurocommunists but for a time had slowly, grudgingly, intermittently made some concessions to them. Moscow did so even though the Eurocommunists developed regional policies (in support of the EEC and even, if only occasionally and partially, of NATO), like Yugoslavia, claimed universal validity for their third way to socialism, and publicly criticized some aspects of Soviet domestic and foreign policy, such as repression of dissidents and Moscow's invasion of Czechoslovakia and Afghanistan.

Soviet polemics with the PCI and the PCE continued. Moscow had unsuccessfully tried to overthrow the PCE's head, Carrillo, whom the PCI supported. Yet there still seemed to be an upward limit to this escalation. Each time the polemics seemed to foreshadow a break, a compromise was reached and the polemics slacked off for a time, only to resume later. Tensions between Moscow and the Eurocommunists were thus cyclical in nature because both felt that they had too much to lose by a break.

Why did the CPSU take Eurocommunism so seriously? Not only because of Soviet state interests, or that plus the CPSU's eroding party empire, but also because in Moscow's view, Eurocommunist theory and practice threatened the domestic legitimacy of the CPSU.

The gerontocratic Soviet leaders probably longed for the good old imperial party days. Because their state empire was expanding, they were the more reluctant to accept that their party empire was declining. Brezhnev, Suslov, and Ponomarev, all in their seventies, rose under Stalin, who had made the Comintern his puppet and decimated the European Communist leaderships. They crushed the Hungarian Revolution in 1956 and the Prague Spring in 1968, they ordered the invasion of Afghanistan, and in mid-1981 they had perhaps only postponed an invasion of Poland. How infuriating, how humiliating it must be for them to make any concessions to the likes of Berlinguer and Carrillo. And how reluctantly, hesitatingly, partially, and infrequently they have done so. A Soviet invasion of Poland would probably end what party relations remain between the CPSU and the PCI and PCE. Barring that, however, Soviet-Eurocommunist relations seemed likely in mid-1981 to remain somewhere between strained correctness and total rupture.

The USSR and the Eurosocialists

Détente intensified contacts between the CPSU and the West European Socialist and Social Democratic parties. The CPSU and even more the Eurocommunists (except the PCF after late 1977) wanted more contacts. As détente went on, most West European socialists (but not the SPD) reciprocated.

The Soviet motive was initially a "popular-front" one: to move the Eurosocialists away from the conservatives toward alliance with the communists. The Eurocommunists' interests were the same, except for Italy recently, where until 1981 the PCI had preferred an alliance with the Christian democrats (the *compromesso storico*).

Two other developments among the socialists favored this tendency: the move toward the left of the French socialists and the revitalization of the Socialist International under the leadership of Willy Brandt and its active support of the noncommunist Left in the Iberian peninsula. Conversely, some Eurosocialists advocated an autonomous, "Gaullo-socialist" European foreign policy vis-à-vis the United States. This attracted the USSR because it was trying since the late 1970s to help worsen U.S.-West European relations, particularly those with Bonn. The SPD saw its *Ostpolitik* threatened in the late 1970s by the decline of détente. The SPD and the USSR, therefore, had a parallel interest to keep détente alive. The USSR wanted to maneuver the SPD into a mediating role between Washington and Moscow.

The USSR also had difficulties with the European socialists. Both refused to make ideological compromises. Moscow tried to prevent the socialists from acquiring ideological influence in Eastern Europe or the USSR itself and was outraged by Eurosocialist support of dissidents there. Moscow also wanted to prevent the socialists from instigating or joining in an anti-Soviet coalition with the Eurocommunists. Finally, Moscow feared the increasing popularity of workers' self-management among the socialists for Eastern Europe was particularly vulnerable to it.

At the end of the 1970s, socialist-communist relations in France differed from those in Italy and Spain. After the brief French socialist–PCF Common Program interlude, in 1977 the PCF returned to its former pro-Soviet, anti–French socialist position.

Nor were Soviet opportunities great with the Italian and Spanish socialists. Craxi, the leader of the Italian Socialist party, turned against the PCI and even more against the USSR. The Spanish Socialist party was so strong, and the PCE so weak, that Gonzáles, the leader of the Spanish socialists, had little to gain from the USSR, to which he was opposed in any case. Thus, in early 1981 the

CPSU's chances with the West European socialists were not good. The Soviets were trying to get the socialists, like West Europeans, to pay for Moscow's helping them to remain an island of détente. Since the West European socialists, and especially, out of a combination of humanitarian and nationalist reasons, the SPD, and also the Eurocommunists gave higher priority to détente than the conservatives did, and since they felt it was menaced by U.S. as well as Soviet policies, Moscow had a Eurosocialist opportunity to exploit.

However, Moscow also had liabilities in Europe—for example, its hostility to the socialist-supported EEC, its repression of dissidents at home, its invasion of Afghanistan, and—for Wester Europe the most alarming—the possibility in 1981 that it would invade Poland. The latter would disrupt Moscow's relations with the socialists and Eurocommunists, who saw in the new independent Polish trade-union movement a workers' initiative against bureaucratized, state-capitalist socialism. Thus, one minimal Soviet aim—control over Eastern Europe—conflicted with a maximal aim—extension of their own influence in Western Europe.

The United States and Eurocommunism

Eurocommunism and, to a lesser extent, Eurosocialism were also issues in U.S. foreign policy. U.S. influence in post-1945 Western Europe was at first overwhelming. In mid-1981 its influence was still great in Italy and West Germany but not in France. U.S. policy in Europe encouraged its unity, its opposition to the USSR, and Franco-German reconciliation. However, as Western Europe revived, its trade and financial competition with the United States, its increasing unwillingness to follow the U.S. lead in foreign economic policy, and its attempts to carry on an autonomous foreign policy alarmed some Americans. This became serious for Washington after France and West Germany refused in 1980 to follow the U.S. lead against the USSR.

Post-1945 U.S. anti-Soviet policy favored conservative parties in Western Europe. Washington especially disliked the SPD's refusal, until 1959, to support NATO and European unity, which it believed would block German reunification and a European security system, and the Italian Socialist party's alliance with the PCI. (The French socialists soon became strongly anticommunist.) Washington also found General de Gaulle's conservative French nationalism very troubling, and in West Germany and Italy the conservatives were weakening. The Kennedy administration supported the Italian *centro-sinistra* (the entry of the Socialist party into the Christian Democrat-dominated government). After the SPD supported NATO and the EEC, Washington's relations with it also improved. Later, however, Henry Kissinger initially distrusted West German *Ostpolitik*, opposed Eurocommunism, and the Eurosocialists priority for détente.

There were three U.S. views in the 1970s about Eurocommunism. The first, led by Kissinger, was hostile. It argued that the Eurocommunists were not becoming social democrats, that their refusal to break their ties with Moscow showed their hostility to the United States, that they opposed most U.S. foreign policy objectives, and that therefore the United States had the right and duty to warn against their policies and to oppose their entry into West European governments. The second, much less-influential, view, held by a few academic specialists on West European communism,[8] argued that the United States should favor the entry of the PCI into the Italian government because otherwise the government could not function; that only a functioning Italy would be an effective U.S. ally; and that the PCI (and the PCE) were moving toward social democracy, had endorsed NATO, and were causing significant trouble to the Soviets. The third view, which I have held, was that while the analysis on which the first view was based was exaggerated and that of the second about the reformism and nationalism of the PCI largely correct, PCI foreign policies were sufficiently opposed to U.S. policies so that its entry into the Italian government was contrary to U.S. interests and that Washington should state this occasionally, moderately, but firmly.

The 1978 electoral defeat of the PCI and the PCF–Socialist party split made the specter of Eurocommunism recede considerably in Washington. The 1980 election of Reagan made it certain that the first policy alternative would be adopted, especially if Eurocommunism should again become more important, and that West European socialists, including the SPD, would be distrusted by his administration.

The Reagan administration's initial negative public reaction to Mitterand's taking four PCF ministers into the new French government showed how strong Washington's opposition to all West European communists was. One main purpose of this declaration was presumably to warn other West European countries of Washington's continued opposition to communist participation in West European governments. Yet its effect in France was primarily to antagonize Mitterand and the French socialists and it showed no realization of the significance of Mitterand's defeat of the PCF.

6

Is Poland Not Yet Lost?

A Self-Limiting Revolution?

The most perilous moment for a government is one when it seeks to mend its ways. Only consummate statecraft can enable a king to save his throne when after a long spell of oppressive rule he sets to improving the lot of his subjects. Patiently endured so long as it seemed beyond redress, a grievance comes to appear intolerable once the possibility of removing it crosses men's minds. For the mere fact that certain abuses have been remedied draws attention to the others and they now appear more galling: people may suffer less, but their sensibility is exacerbated. —Alexis de Tocqueville[1]

Poland is the USSR's most important ally because of its geographical location on the historic invasion route to Moscow, its size, and its resources. Fiercely nationalist, devoutly Catholic, and traditional fighters for their freedom from Russia, Poland is also the ally Moscow finds most difficult to dominate. If the USSR lost all its influence over Poland, it would face the loss of East Germany, German reunification, and global encirclement. Yet Poland's agriculture has been overwhelmingly private since 1956, and the Roman Catholic church has long been its source of real authority (*pays réel*) and the Communist party only its government (*pays légal*). Uniquely in Eastern Europe, three times before—in 1956, 1970, and 1976—when communist control seemed endangered, the Red Army did *not* invade Poland.[2]

For the first time in any communist country, in late summer 1980, Polish workers won an independent, legally institutionalized trade-union movement by nonviolent sit-down strikes, the most difficult trade-union tactic for communists—or capitalists—to combat. Their victory, an event perhaps even more important than the Soviet-Yugoslav break, endangered Moscow's global position for if it, or most of it, were to last, it would probably gradually infect the rest of Eastern Europe and later perhaps even the non–Great Russian nations in the USSR. If the Red Army crushed it, however, Moscow would lose its hopes to gain in Western Europe and drive the United States further into cold war and alliance with, and the arming of, China.

Note: *Jeszcze Polska nie zgineła* ("Poland is not yet lost") is the opening line of the Polish national anthem.

The 1980 Polish workers' victory was one of the few unifying events in modern Polish history that had centered in part on the struggle between "reds" and "whites"—those who wanted to revolt against Russia and those who did not. The modern Polish intelligentsia was also split between practicing Catholics and agnostic leftists. The workers' 1980 victory temporarily surmounted these splits, which only the independence struggles during both world wars had done before, by creating a symbiosis of nationalism, Catholicism, and Christian and social democracy. Most important, it gave Polish society more elbow room for its protracted struggle with the Communist party.

By 1980 this struggle was in its second round. The first round had ended in 1968 when a wave of intellectual and student discontent had played into the hands of General Mieczysław Moczar, then the leader of the ambitious, antisemitic partisans. His attempt to take power failed when Gomułka got Brezhnev's support after the invasion of Czechoslovakia. The second round had begun in December 1970 with workers' demonstrations in the Polish seacoast cities, sparked by meat price increases, in which many workers were killed. Gomułka fell prey to a palace revolt headed by Edward Gierek and aided by Moczar, whom Gierek soon purged.

In 1976, workers' demonstrations broke out, triggered again by rises in meat prices. As it had in 1970, the communist leadership gave in to most of the workers' demands but did not carry out many of them. Thus for the first time in history, a Communist party twice gave in to workers' demands and then backtracked on its concessions. The workers thus learned that they could block price increases and overthrow a party head but that they had to institutionalize their victory.

The workers had grown accustomed in the early 1970s to rising living standards, only to see them fade in the late 1970s. They were determined to keep them from declining more and were confident they could do so. By 1980, Polish workers were very different from those in the 1950s and 1960s. They were better educated, disciplined, modernized, wholly disillusioned with reforms from above and with the party leadership that they saw as their exploiters, and deeply nationalist and Catholic. They comprised a modern, mature working class with successful experience in strikes, the beginnings of a spontaneous trade-union leadership, and a trade-union ideology that evolved out of their experience and that was elaborated by dissident intellectuals.

After 1970, Gierek borrowed billions from the West to modernize Polish industry and thus make its exports competitive in the world market and to import food and consumer goods to raise living standards. Workers' real wages and expectations rose rapidly during the first half of the 1970s, far faster than productivity. Then the Polish economy went sour. Some causes were external: for example, rising energy costs, including Soviet petroleum, and costlier imports from the West. Poland imported and suffered from Western inflation and stagflation, which cut back Polish exports. However, most causes were domestic.

For example, capital investments were too great to be fully productive. They also cut back on consumer-goods production, a move that thus led to massive unsatisfied demand. Because private farmers did not get enough aid, agricultural productivity remained low. Poland therefore had to import great amounts of food. Because there were no basic economic reforms, industrial productivity was even lower. Gierek then cut back imports, which only worsened the situation further. Poland had to borrow even more in the West including, by the late 1970s, money to pay for its huge debt service. (Because Schmidt wanted to preserve *Ostpolitik* and was close to Gierek, he urged the West German banks to extend new loans.)

Many Polish communist officials became bourgeois in their living styles. They were Mafialike in their corruption, softened by special stores where they could cheaply buy Western goods and by country *dachas* where they could enjoy themselves out of sight of the working class whose vanguard they claimed to be, and cynical about their discredited ideology. They thus became less likely to risk revolution or even trouble by resisting worker or intelligentsia pressure. Gierek's policies benefited the scientific and technical intelligentsia much more than the workers.

At the end of the 1970s, the Polish economic crisis worsened rapidly. Poland's debt to the West was $14 billion at the end of 1978 and $25 billion by 1981. Net national income fell 2 percent in 1980, and inflation was estimated at 8 percent. Economic growth, the rate of increase of consumption, and upward social mobility declined.

A major crisis of political authority ensued because nothing creates a revolutionary situation so rapidly or decisively as the disappointment of rising mass expectations plus the demonstrated unwillingness of a repressive but decaying and delegitimized regime to crush the mass discontent that it generates.

The 1970 and 1976 demonstrations produced new leaders who were thereafter harassed but not kept out of circulation by the regime and who were eager for new opportunities. In late 1977, several unofficial free trade-union cells were set up, of which the most important was the Free Baltic Trade Union in Gdańsk. One of its founding members was a young, devoutly Catholic electrician, Lech Wałęca, who had been a member of the 1970 strike committee there and who was often fired and arrested thereafter. He and others like him had come into touch with the dissident intellectuals through their publications, notably *Robotnik*, founded by KSS/KOR members (see below) for workers in 1977. Wałęca became one of the editors of the Free Baltic Trade Union paper, *Robotnik Wybrzeza*.[3]

The Church

Polish nationalism and Catholicism have historically been as integrally and indissolubly a whole as they have been in Ireland. From 1795 to 1918, while

Poland was partitioned, the Roman Catholic church was the only institution that incarnated and sustained the Polish struggle for national survival and independence. The church's heroic World War II resistance against the Nazis and the Soviets and its quiet, determined refusal after 1945 to collaborate with the Soviet and Polish communists reinforced its historic role.

From World War II until June 1981 the Polish church was headed by the late great Polish patriot and ecclesiastical statesman, Stefan Cardinal Wyszyński. The election of its other great leader, Karol Cardinal Wojtyła of Cracow, as Pope John Paul II and his triumphal visit in 1979 to his native land, during which the self-imposed discipline of the overwhelming crowds was in retrospect a rehearsal for the discipline of the 1980 strikes, further confirmed the church's leadership of Poland. Remember the Pope's picture on the gates of the Gdańsk Shipyard during the 1980 strike; the crowds of workers thronging Catholic masses and confessions there; and Wałęca, holding a crucifix, signing the strikers' agreement with the government with a huge red and white pen (the Polish colors) distributed during the Pope's visit. True, Cardinal Wyszyński's speech during the strike underestimated, many thought, how much the workers could safely hope to gain, but the immediately following Episcopate declaration caught up with events. The Cardinal's early September 1980 audience for Wałęca and his associates, after offering a mass for them in his private chapel, his subsequent endorsements of their activities, and the increasingly active role of the church in mediating strike settlements showed again that the church/worker symbiosis was alive and well in all of Poland.[4]

Catholic and Revisionist Dissidence before 1970

The defeat of the noncommunist Polish resistance in the 1944 Warsaw rising and the glacier of Stalinist terror thereafter temporarily submerged Polish resistance to Soviet rule. However, liberal Catholic intellectuals who tried to modernize the church, which before 1939 had been dogmatic and chauvinist and often antisemitic, revived the nineteenth-century ideology of political realism or organic work, which patriotic Poles had developed after the tsars crushed the great Polish risings of 1830 and 1863—that is, limited cooperation with the occupying powers to further Poland's economic development. This policy, supported by Cardinal Wyszyński, was formulated by Stanisław Stomma and his associates in the liberal Catholic *Znak* publishing group and spread by the Cracow Catholic weekly, *Tygodnik Powszechny*. In 1956 Gomułka came to terms with the church and coopted several of these anti-Marxist but not anti-Soviet Catholic intellectuals into parliament. As Gomułka's and later Gierek's Thermidor proceeded, however, their position gradually eroded and they were maneuvered out of political life, which culminated in Stomma's lone vote against the 1975 pro-Soviet amendments to the Polish constitution—a symbolic rejection of collaboration compared, when he did it, to Rejtan, the Polish parliamentarian who lay down across the door of the parliament at the end of the eighteenth century to protest its acceptance of Poland's partition.

By 1980, most liberal Catholics were thus disillusioned with cooperation with the Communist party, had several publications (for example, *Tygodnik Powszechny* and *Więź*), a publishing house (*Znak*), and several clubs of Catholic intellectuals (KIK), and they were ready to shift to pressure from below. In 1980, some of them became involved in the burgeoning workers' discontent and were prominent among the experts advising Solidarity during the August 1980 strikes. One of these, Tadeusz Maziowecki, editor-in-chief of *Więź*, later became editor of Solidarity's newspaper.

The Polish communist revisionists of the 1950s and 1960s had been pushed toward social democracy by Gomułka's and Gierek's rejection of all their demands for reform. The final blow to their hopes came in 1968, when not only was a wave of intellectual and student discontent ruthlessly suppressed but also antisemitism became for a time the main weapon of repression. Thereafter many of them, now ex-revisionists, concluded that they had no hope for improvement unless they allied with the church and the Catholic intellectuals. The December 1970 strike and the party's concessions to the workers convinced the revisionists that any successful protest movement must have a working-class base, which meant alliance with the church.

The *Znak* and the revisionists left an important heritage. They had brought renewed political consciousness and maturity to the Polish intelligentsia. They had shown that cooperation with a communist leadership did not work. Because the revisionists lost faith in Marxism, and the leftist Catholic intelligentsia helped to make the church's anticommunism politically more sophisticated, they prepared the way for the new ideology of pressure from below.

Intellectual Dissidence after 1970

Intellectuals, communist and not, had been in the forefront of the previous waves of East European unrest. (Only in the Plzeň and East Berlin spontaneous workers' risings had it been the workers themselves.) Ferment had begun among disaffected communist activists and had spread to party intellectuals, then to students and the communication media, and finally to the workers. It had begun as ideologically revisionist—that is, it tried to turn back from the distortions of Stalinism to true Leninism or true Marxism.

By 1980, however, belief in Marxism-Leninism was almost dead in Poland. Socialism, in the sense of continued nationalization of heavy industry plus massive social welfare, was accepted. The workers did not want to return to pre-1939 capitalism for socialism had brought them job security and a leisurely pace of work, but the privileges and corruption of the regime and the declining living standards of the population made dissident intellectuals and workers more egalitarian. Polish dissidence after 1968, when Gomułka crushed revisionist intellectual and student opposition, was Christian or social democratic, not revisionist, and strongly nationalist.

After the 1976 strikes, two new dissident groups developed. Far from being clandestine, they constantly and publicly declared their motives and their aims. One leftist, non-Catholic group, KSS/KOR, was made up of oppositional intellectuals who had either always been social democrats, or excommunists, like Jacek Kuroń and Adam Michnik, who later became social democrats. Another group, ROPCiO, was more nationalist and Catholic. (A third, clandestine group, PPN, which called for the overthrow of the regime, had little influence.) By summer 1980, Polish dissidents were publishing more than thirty regular, uncensored newspapers and magazines, with circulations in the thousands and a mass audience of millions through their rebroadcast by Radio Free Europe.[5] The World War II "Flying University" also revived—that is, dissident professors lectured to eager students, as did the Student Solidarity Committee (SKS). The police often harassed these groups, sometimes briefly imprisoned their leaders, but never suppressed them.

The dissidents tried to build up other pressure groups; to mobilize international opinion in their support; to set up independent sources of information and analysis; to publish noncensored publications; to have their publications, and thereby their ideology, broadcast back into Poland, primarily by Radio Free Europe, and thereby gradually to create a counterculture.

KSS/KOR's and ROPCiO's key contributions to the 1980 strikes were twofold. KSS/KOR members published a semimonthly paper, *Robotnik* ("The Worker"—the name of the pre-1939 daily of the Polish Socialist party), which by summer 1980 printed up to 50,000 copies. Its editorial board had representatives from all major Polish industrial centers, and its ideas influenced the burgeoning free trade-union leadership.[6] For example, *Robotnik* wrote in May 1980:

> Action in defense of arrested workers is essential, especially by their co-workers. If other methods fail, one can resort to strikes.

> The demands of each strike must contain, in addition to economic matters, specific demands for an end to political repression as well.[7]

Robotnik also published an action program of specific demands. ROPCiO helped organize semilegal free trade unions on the Baltic seacoast, notably in Gdańsk.

The one semidissident organization, which included party as well as nonparty members, was the DiP ("Experience and the Future"). Even this was not primarily Marxist revisionist because many of the party members in it had also become convert social democrats. In 1979 and 1980, before the August 1980 strikes, DiP sent two major in-system reformist analyses of the Polish situation to the party leadership that provided detailed, sophisticated analyses of the Polish political and economic crises.[8] Their contents were broadcast back into Poland by Radio Free Europe so they received something like mass circulation. There was reportedly some sympathy with the DiP ideas at the highest levels of the party, but the ideas never were put into practice.

These dissident groups, with the partial exception of DiP, had a nonclass orientation—that is, they appealed to all social strata. They stressed popular appeal, consensus, and concerted, organized activity. They tried to learn from their experience and from the 1970 and 1976 strikes. With the exception of PPN, they opposed conspiratorial activity or challenge to the leading role of the Communist party or the alliance of Poland with the USSR. Far from wanting to remain in the ghetto of the intelligentsia, they tried hard to establish contacts with dissident workers and peasants and gradually succeeded. Their ultimate objectives were free trade unions for workers and peasants, near total end of censorship and of discrimination against Christians, and student participation in their own affairs.

They had become social democrats for a somewhat different reason from the one that made revolutionary Marxists become social democrats in Imperial Germany or within the Eurocommunist Western Communist parties after 1968, both of whom had embraced parliamentary gradualism rather than revolution because they otherwise saw no chance of electoral victory. The Polish non-Catholic dissidents became social democrats not only because they had lost faith in Marxism, or always had been social democrats, but also because they knew that the Red Army would crush any attempt to overthrow communism in Poland or even the sort of Marxist revisionism that had been widespread in Poland and Hungary in 1956 and in Czechoslovakia in 1968. In-system self-limited reforms of Polish communism, without challenging its ideology, leading role, or ties with Moscow, was thus for them politics as the art of the possible.

The new ideology, which played a major role in the 1980 strikes and thereafter, was first developed in detail primarily by the non-Catholic dissidents—notably, Adam Michnik, a young excommunist historian who had been imprisoned after 1968 and who then became the private secretary of the famous writer Antoni Słonimski and later the principal KSS/KOR ideologist, and Jacek Kuroń, another excommunist who became KSS/KOR's organizational leader. This ideology had at its core the mobilization of nonconspiratorial but not formally legal dissident groups who in turn would mobilize society against the state by creating nonlegal trade-union cells, student organizations, and peasant unions. It was initially gradualist and reformist for it accepted the impossibility, given Soviet policy, of a multiparty system or ending the alliance with the USSR. However, it maintained that the USSR eventually be brought to accept such a development because it would realize that the cost of intervention would be greater and that developments would remain controlled and limited. The movement would be based on the working class, which alone could achieve the ideology's goal. The intellectuals allied with the church, which had supported the workers in the 1970 strikes. (The new ideology thus proposed an end to the traditional Polish split between the church and the secular left.) As Kuroń put it:

> Open protest, synchronized in a number of centers, unites the country and becomes a social movement . . . a joint form of action in which every participant realizes his aims by acting in a small, independent group.[9]

In the face of the developing opposition, the more-pragmatic party members and leaders favored some compromises with it, but as Michnik put it, they could at most be partners but never allies.[10]

The Communist Party

In 1980, the party leadership, discredited and disunited by factional struggles, was nearly rent apart by the strike. It had been split among a few genuine reformers such as Rakowski, Jagielski, Barczikowski, and Fiszbach; pragmatic, reluctant, only economic reformers like Olszowski and Kania; hard-liners such as Łukasiewicz, who wanted more repression; and Gierek, trapped in between. In February, for reasons of personal rivalry, Gierek ousted Olszowski and made Babiuch, another reluctant, pragmatic economic reformer, prime minister. Babiuch's partial reforms, sabotaged by hard-liners, could not contain the deepening crisis. Party writers and intellectuals were openly critical.[11] When the seacoast strikes broke out in July 1980, Gierek initially offered minimal concessions and sacrificed Babiuch and Łukasiewicz. Thereafter, when the strikes spread, the most pragmatic economic reformers, Jagielski and Barczikowski, successfully negotiated with the workers and became more powerful and Gierek's position rapidly eroded. After the strike ended, Gierek had a heart attack, as Gomułka had just before he fell in 1970, and Kania, with Minister of Defense General Jaruzelski (who had opposed the use of force against the strikers), replaced him.

The 1980 Strikes and Their Results

> What must seem still more extraordinary to us, given our experience of the aftermath of so many revolutions, is that the possibility of a violent upheaval never crossed our parents' minds.[12]

The strikes began locally, sparked by the July 1980 meat price rises. At first the strikers concentrated on getting financial compensation for the price rises, which the workers believed broke the party's commitment to them, rather than on having them reversed. Unlike the 1970 and 1976 strikes when party head-quarters had been burned down, the 1980 strikes were sit-down and entirely peaceful. *Robotnik* had spread KSS/KOR's slogan, "Form committees, don't burn them." The historic memories of the slaughter of the risings of 1830, 1863, and 1944; the Soviet invasions of Hungary and Czechoslovakia; and the workers' mature trade-union consciousness also restrained the strikers.[13] Indeed, they were so peaceful, so disciplined, and so wholly sit-down in charac-ter that the party leadership, which initially reacted slowly and indecisively, saw no alternative but to restrain itself in return. At first the workers' demands were economic only, and dissident intellectuals were not involved. Their role was limited to informing the foreign press about strikes and thereby assuring that news of them (which the party suppressed) be broadcast back into Poland by Radio Free Europe. The party leadership did not imagine that such spon-taneous local strikes could produce an organized, nationwide strike movement and initially hoped to handle them at the local level.

The second phase, also spontaneous, was one of large-scale organization of the strikers, and it began in August, primarily on the seacoast. The Lenin Shipyard at Gdańsk, which had been one of the centers of the 1970 strikes, took the lead in forming a regional organization, MKS, under the watchword *solidarity,* which symbolized the priority of unity. The MKS soon added political and institutional demands. The Gdańsk-strike leadership initially was ready to end the strike after the management agreed to higher wages, the reinstatement of two dismissed workers, and a monument to the workers killed in the Decem-ber 1970 strike, but the workers themselves demanded that the strike continue. The initial political demands went very far indeed and included free elections, but the Gdańsk KSS/KOR representative and the Catholic experts achieved their limitation to their rights to strike, free expression, release and rehabilita-tion of political prisoners, publication of the establishment of the MKS and of its demands, information about Poland's economic situation, and debate about reform, wage increases, the elimination of special shops, and a five-day work week. These demands, which rapidly spread throughout Poland, became the workers' program in negotiations with the government.

Initially the government tried to harass and isolate the MKS. It cut off all communications to Gdańsk and denounced them as antisocialist. None-theless KSS/KOR kept the foreign press informed, and Radio Free Europe broadcast their reports back to Poland so the party's communication blockage failed. The MKS remained firm and tension escalated throughout Poland. Cardinal Wyszyński and a group of intellectuals, fearful of an explosion, called for calm and reason. The Cardinal had underestimated the workers' determina-tion, however. He soon took a stronger stand, as did the episcopate, and Catholic and non-Catholic intellectual dissidents were invited by the MKS to advise it. They played an important role in the final negotiations. The government had arrested the principal leaders of KSS/KOR, which was therefore initially not represented among the experts. Realizing that compromise was inevitable, and after General Jaruzelski declared that Polish soldiers would not fire on workers, the leadership sent Kazimierz Barcikowski and Mieczysław Jagielski to negotiate with the MKS in Szczecin and Gdańsk respectively.[14] Four Politburo members—including Prime Minister Babiuch and agitprop chief Łukasiewicz and trade-union head Szydlak, both hard-liners—were replaced by Olszowski and Grabski. Gierek was replaced by Kania shortly thereafter.

The final agreement, on 31 August, was a landmark in post-1945 Polish history. It was a major victory for the workers, and thereby for society, against the party and state. All the workers' demands were accepted. In return they agreed only that the party played the leading role in the state and that Poland's alliance with the USSR was inviolable. (This concession was made by Wałęca at the urging of the Catholic experts.) He overruled the radical workers and some KSS/KOR sympathizers. (Thus the first confrontation began to repolarize the Catholics versus KSS/KOR.) The government also agreed that the workers had the right to strike, that all political prisoners including the KSS/KOR leaders would be immediately released, that censorship would be rigidly restricted, and that Catholic mass would be broadcast on Sunday. The economic egalitarian part of the agreement included a gradual increase in wages, particularly for the lowest paid workers; a slowdown of consumer price increases; and cutbacks on special privileges, special sales, stores, and so forth.

By mid-1981, five main political poststrike developments in the Polish *odnowa* ("renewal") stood out: (1) the attempt of Solidarity and groups of writers, students, and peasants to deepen and institutionalize political pluralism in Poland; (2) the attempt of the party leadership to check and begin to reverse this trend;[15] (3) the renewed polarization between moderates (the Catholics) and radicals (KSS/KOR) within and without Solidarity; (4) the attempt of the Communist-party base to renew its leadership and apparat; and (5) the indecision of Moscow about whether to crush Polish political pluralism by force.

Solidarity Versus Party

The pattern that emerged in the continuing struggle between the free trade union and the party was one of recurrent crises with mutual brinkmanship's giving way to compromise once tension reached the point at which both sides believed that a Soviet invasion was at hand. The four major crises occurred (1) in autumn 1980 about the legal registration of Solidarity,[16] followed in December by the impressive, Catholic dedication of a monument in Gdańsk to the workers killed in the 1970 strikes, a symbol of affirmation of national identity and the need for national reconciliation;[17] (2) in January 1981 about the five-day week;[18] (3) in February about peasants' and students' unions; and (4) in late March about the Bydgoszcz "provocation" (see below). The government vacillated on the first crisis; it first had a court amend the registration application and then the Supreme Court reverse it. Intermittent waves of strikes showed how serious the situation was and that few alternatives were left. In early December 1980, the White House let it be known that a Soviet invasion of Poland was imminent, and the Polish party leadership strongly implied the same. Then, however, for reasons we do not know, Brezhnev decided not to invade.

Wałęca's position was becoming more difficult. He, the church, and most Catholic and social-democratic intellectuals, fearful of invasion, pleaded for moderation against the radicals in Solidarity's leadership and, increasingly, in KSS/KOR who wanted to take a harder line largely because they thought that a Soviet invasion was very unlikely. As other social groups reemerged and pluralism progressed, Wałęca's influence was increasingly challenged, and the Polish political scene became more fragmented.

Attempts of other social strata to institutionalize pluralism began (as they had in previous waves of liberalization in Eastern Europe before August 1980) with university students. In late 1980, student strikes in universities, centering in Łódź, became nationwide. The strikers won a nearly complete victory in February 1981. The egalitarian and libertarian agreement recognized a free students' union (NZS). Student representatives were to make up one-third of the university and faculty councils, and their powers would be greatly increased. Censorship of academic publications was to be ended. Marxism-Leninism and Russian-language courses would no longer be compulsory, and history books would be revised.[19]

A similar process took place in the journalists' and writers' unions. The previous conformist journalists' leadership was replaced by a largely noncommunist one headed by the leader of DiP, Stefan Bratkowski, a reformist communist. The Writers Union elected the Catholic Jan Józef Szczepański as its new head and took a strong stand against previous party practices.[20]

Peasants were setting up a rural Solidarity. There had been indications of this, aided by KSS/KOR, before the August 1980 strikes. The independent peasants' union, first set up on 10 September 1978, was a direct descendant of various local peasants' committees and indeed indirectly of the pre-1939 Polish peasant party (PSL.) Several unofficial peasant publications began to appear, and a peasant university was set up. The original peasants' organizing committee was close to ROPCiO and later to KSS/KOR. During the summer 1980 strikes, it endorsed the strikers' demands and demanded that the right to free organization be extended to peasants.[21] Conversely, on 22 September 1980, Solidarity declared that the Gdańsk agreement covered all workers in agriculture, including individual peasant proprietors.

After the August 1980 strikes, peasant activity burgeoned despite strong party opposition. In early 1981, the peasant organization was active but had not been registered. In mid-February 1981, the government came to terms with two striking peasant unions in Rzeszow and Istrzyki Dolne "acting in the name of the founding national committee of the professional union of individual peasants." Wałęca and another Solidarity representative and the episcopate secretary, Bishop Dąbrowski, participated and mediated in the negotiations. The right of private peasant proprietors to their lands was legally recognized. A national peasant union was legally registered in May 1981 as one of the results of the post-Bydgoszcz compromise, despite communist fears that it would be in fact a renewal of the traditional PSL, with strong Christian Democratic tendencies. Substantively, the agreement was more detailed than the one with Solidarity. It was a large-scale victory for Rural Solidarity, notably by the government's agreement to increase aid to agriculture and to divide it between private and collectivized and state agriculture according to the areas cultivated— that is, the end of financial discrimination against private agriculture. Moreover, private peasants would be free to buy and sell land, and their farms would not be limited in size. The two other small legal parties, the United Peasant and Democratic parties, rapidly transformed themselves into more genuine ones, but they were too small and discredited to play a major role.

Poland in fact had four parties in mid-1981, of which the only legal one, the Communist party, was the weakest and most split. The other three, the church, Solidarity, and Rural Solidarity, were in the ironic, paradoxical position of feeling compelled to try to prop up the legal Communist party, as well as to further its renewal, lest the latter be crushed by the Red Army.

The church became stronger vis-à-vis Solidarity and the party leadership. The primate's initial hesitation to endorse the strike gave way to strong support of Solidarity and within it to support of Wałęca and the moderate majority against the radicals and KSS/KOR. For the party, the church had become the indispensable force for restraint by the working class and the country. The Pope also endorsed Solidarity, but in general terms. Basically, he remained in reserve, ready, presumably, to throw his overwhelming prestige into the scales if he deemed the situation critical enough.

KSS/KOR, although it officially dissolved itself in September 1980, continued active, denounced by the party leadership and the Soviet and East European press.[22] At first, after the August 1980 strike, it pursued its prestrike policy—namely, gradualist, limited reforms guaranteed by institutionalized social pluralism and acceptance of the leading role of the Communist party and Poland's alliance with the USSR.[23] By mid-1981, however, the attitude of KSS/KOR's leader, Kuroń, and of its chief ideologist, Michnik, had become more radical. They and the radical Solidarity leaders declared that contrary to the views of the primate, Wałęca, and the Catholic and social-democratic advisors, only continued pressure and greater demands could prevent the party from reversing the revolution's gains and that to do this was feasible because it was very unlikely that the USSR would invade Poland. Although Kuroń and

Michnik continued to have considerable influence on Solidarity activists, the radical line was defeated in all the confrontations within Solidarity's leadership; its key experts, and above all the church, increasingly opposed it; and polarization in and around Solidarity and among its experts thus increased.

At first the party leadership intended to do what it had done in 1956, 1970, and 1976: to procrastinate, split the opposition, and thus erode what the August 1980 strike had achieved. But this time it did not succeed. On the contrary, it was driven to further retreats vis-à-vis the church, Solidarity, and Rural Solidarity. What was left of its fragile authority eroded further. By mid-1981, what the party leadership had left was the national consensus that it had to be kept, and even propped up, in its leading role in order to prevent a Soviet invasion, plus Kania's resistance to Soviet pressure.

By then the party itself, and the revolt of its base against the apparat and leadership, had become a central problem of Polish politics. Central because, first, the church, Solidarity, Rural Solidarity, and the party leadership—and the Soviets—had come to a temporary compromise at the end of March 1981 and the beginning of April 1981, after the Bydgoszcz provocation, and therefore the spotlight shifted to the struggle within the party. Second, Solidarity seemed for the time being ready to consolidate its gains and to prepare for a second provocation. The rank-and-file party members—workers and technical intelligentsia—wanted to rehabilitate themselves; reformist party intellectuals such as Rakowski, Bratkowski, and the party members in DiP had drawn up specific proposals for reform of the party; and a few of the apparat decided that since they could not lick them they had better join them as did a few in the party leadership.[24] These developments were highlighted in mid-April 1981 by a meeting in Toruń of horizontal committees of elected party representatives from factories in various key regions—a *dvoevlastie* ["double-power"] within the party itself—that demanded that the present party leadership be renewed almost completely, that the censorship no longer ban mention of the activists' efforts, that the delegates to the forthcoming party congress be elected by secret ballot, that the party central committee inform other socialist countries of the real situation in Poland, and that the ties among these horizontal committees be institutionalized. Their leaders reportedly were talking at Torun of allowing at most 20 percent of the old central committee to remain—but only if the party leadership would agree to such a deal with them at once. Thus the party leadership, which felt compelled at the late-March 1981 central committee plenum to promise that a party congress would be held no later than 20 July 1981, was faced by early May by what amounted to an attempt by the newly-organized party base to replace much of it and of the apparat, by a renewed alternative. The April visit of Suslov to Warsaw demonstrated the grave Soviet concern about these developments but did not immediately presage decisive Soviet action against them.

The Economy

The Polish economy continued to worsen after the August 1980 strikes, in part because of them and the subsequent confusion and erosion of authority. National income was projected to be 2 percent lower than planned for the second year running. Industrial production was running 17 percent less than it did in 1979. Productions losses were estimated to be 70 billion złoty (2.3 billion). Construction was down 44 percent and coal exports down 25 percent. Agricultural production was also down: potatoes 40 percent and meat 33 percent.[25] The wage increases that the party had conceded to the workers in the August 1980 agreement fueled inflation, increased budget deficits, and pushed up purchasing power, but the strike-caused shortfall in production made their control more difficult. Thus from a purely economic viewpoint, another price rise was necessary, but politically it could be near suicidal. Because the strike leaders and the party recognized this, they supported meat rationing to allot it fairly, prevent profiteering, and thus try to slow down the erosion of political stability. Economic reforms were proposed, modelled more on Hungary than on Yugoslavia.[26]

The USSR, the United States, and the European economic community increased their credits to Poland and promised food aid. The Western governments postponed Poland's repayments on their previous loans to Poland. The Western banks, however, continued to negotiate the terms of any postponement. Poland was by mid-1981 perilously close to massive default on its bank loans. Moreover, at its early July 1981 Sofia meeting, Comecon refused to give any more credits to Poland. Thus the 1981 Polish economic situation was desperate and no relief was in sight. Moreover, productivity had fallen drastically and the collapse of the party's authority and the wage increases which Solidarity had won made the economic situation worse still.

Finally, we come to the highly professionalized Polish armed forces. During the crucial leadership discussions in August 1980, General Jaruzelski made clear—as he had in 1976 after, in his view, the army had been demoralized by firing on the workers in 1970—that the Polish army would never again shoot on Polish workers. Moreover, by early 1981, several hundred thousand new draftees had entered the army who had gone through the same experiences as the rest of the country, so they were even less likely to shoot than before. Still, whether they would or not remained less important than whether Brezhnev thought that they would.[27]

A key question thus became whether the party, the church, the workers' leaders, and the oppositional intellectuals, or at least the first three of them, could prevent something close to anarchy or hunger riots and thus become the moral guarantors of the settlements reached in August 1980 and thereafter. (Indeed, the church became *the* mediator among and within all contending social groups, including the party.[28] Then Minister of Defense General Jaruzelski replaced Pinkowski as prime minister. One of the most reformist members of the party central committee, Mieczysław Rakowski, the editor-in-chief of *Polityka*, became deputy prime minister in charge of labor and information. That Moczar became deputy prime minister was disquieting (until he had a heart attack), and Olszowski and Grabski, previously purged by Ochab in part because they had pressed for some pragmatic economic reforms, became the leaders of the pro-Soviet hard-liners.[29] Jaruzelski's call for ninety days without strikes was only initially followed.

Shortly after Jaruzelski's appointment, the peasant and student strikes were settled on terms very favorable to them. Plans were announced for rationing meat and some other foodstuffs. Drafts of new party statutes emphasized democratization of the party and an upper limit on party members' incomes. Rakowski declared that the censorship would rapidly be limited. Kania visited Prague and East Berlin and then Moscow, where he attended the twenty-sixth Soviet party congress, and Moscow and the West both postponed payments on the Polish debt.[30]

Then, in mid-March 1981, the Byzgoszcz provocation threatened a general strike and a Soviet invasion. Several hundred police broke into a sit-down strike there and badly beat up several participants, including Rulewski, the regional head of Solidarity. (It was assumed in Warsaw that Polish hard-liners, perhaps with Soviet help or urging, had organized the provocation—far from the first, and certainly not the last, in Polish history.)

The radical Solidarity activists and the KSS/KOR leaders demanded a general strike in protest. Wałęca, the church, and the moderate advisors opposed it on the ground that it would mean a Soviet invasion. A compromise was reached between Wałęca and Rakowski only a few hours before the general strike was scheduled to begin. Instead, there was a disciplined four-hour warning strike throughout Poland. However, Wałęca had to exert all his authority, and that of the primate, to prevent a general strike; Rakowski used all his influence on the party leadership; and presumably, they in turn used their influence on Brezhnev to get Solidarity, the party, and Brezhnev to accept the compromise. At the subsequent 9 March plenum of the party central committee, the moderate line prevailed, but despite strong attacks on him, the hard-line Olszowski (and Grabski) remained in the Politburo, presumably as part of the early-April 1981 Soviet decision not to invade Poland.[31] Had the threat of a general strike not been averted, a few hours before it would have begun, a Soviet invasion, for which all preparations, as in December 1980, had been made, would probably have begun.

Another brief period of relative quiet ensued. Then on 5 June, after the hard-liners began to agitate against Kania and some (probably provocative) desecrations of Soviet monuments occurred, the CPSU sent a stern, threatening letter to the Polish central committee. It denounced Kania and Jaruzelski by name for losing control of the Polish communist party, which, Moscow maintained, was therefore threatened, by revisionists within it and the counter-revolution outside it, with collapse as a Marxist-Leninist party. The letter's purpose, like that of the Bydgoszcz provocation, was to bring about the replacement of the party leadership by a hard-line group which would crack down on the Polish renewal and, if Moscow felt necessary, ask for Soviet military intervention. Presumably with Soviet foreknowledge and approval, Tadeusz Grabski, a hard-line extremist, at a central committee meeting which Kania immediately called, led a move to unseat Kania. But by a combination of extraordinary tactical finesse, the support of the generals and provincial secretaries present, and the prudent refusal of Olszowski to join Grabski, Kania beat back the attack.

In the weeks immediately thereafter Kania showed even greater tactical skill by his moderation in victory. Indeed, he even intervened to get Grabski, Olszowski, and Zabiński (another hard-liner) elected as delegates to the congress, in order to appease the Soviets, restrain the radicals, and try to coopt as many hard-liners as possible to his centrist camp. He also brought the press under more control.

Meanwhile, by early July the elections of delegates to the party congress, which after the Toruń meeting had seemed likely to bring a victory of the radical reformers, swung in favor of Kania's centrist line. They also reflected the massive personnel changes in the party apparat, the result of the democratic reform wave of the party base. For example, 80 percent of the old central committee members were not elected delegates and most of the regional party officials were replaced. But the delegates' composition was to Kania's advantage, since some of the radical reformers were defeated and most of the hard-liners were elected because of Kania's intervention in their favor. Several factors contributed to the centrist victory: the Soviet pressure, directly and through Kania's use of it against the radical reformers; Kania's victory at the June plenum, which greatly strengthened his authority; the radicals' use of Solidarity rather than the party for their main activity; and, perhaps, the beginning of the ebbing of revolutionary fervor. In addition, the Pope's early July designation of Bishop Józef Glemp, a long-time associate of Cardinal Wyszyński, who died the month before, as Archbishop of Gniezno and Warsaw, indicated that the Church would continue its mediating role.

The 14–20 July party congress was indeed, as it was termed, extraordinary, and paradoxical as well. It was remarkably democratic and far from controlled by Kania. It resulted in an unexpected and unprecedented renewal of the central committee and the politburo. It consolidated the control of the centrists over the party leadership and diminished the influence of both the hard-liners and the reformists.

Above all, it was a victory of the base over all except the very top of the apparat. Out of the 200 members of the new central committee, 80 were workers and 28 peasants, a far larger percentage of both than before. Only 18 out of the 142 members of the old central committee were reelected. The new central committee included only 4 of the 11 members of the old politburo, 3 out of 9 of the old party secretariat, 8 out of 49 provincial party secretaries, and none of the 17 old central committee department heads.

The defeat of the hard-liners was nearly complete: Grabski, Żabiński, Kociołek, and even Moczar were not elected to the new central committee. But such reformers as Fiszbach, first secretary of Gdansk, and Dąbrowa, first secretary of Cracow, were also defeated. Olszowski, who had become a moderate conservative, was barely elected; so was Rakowski, whose congress speech, an eloquent call for continued reforms, had electrified the delegates.

Kania got two third of the delegates' votes for the central committee. (Only Jaruzelski got more.) However, his attempt to be elected at the beginning of the congress failed—one of the many signs that the delegates refused to be manipulated by anyone.

Kania also got two thirds of the votes for first secretary, after two of the others nominated by the new central committee, Olszowski and Rakowski, declined and the third, Kania's close ally Barcikowski, ran only to have another candidate presented. The new Politburo included only four of the previous members: Kania, Jaruzelski, Barcikowski, and Olszowski. Four workers were added, including one woman member of Solidarity (Grzyb), one reformer (Labecki), and one outspoken hard-liner (Siwak). Also added were two ministers (Czyrek of foreign affairs and Milewski of interior), two academics, and three regional secretaries (Rakowski was not elected).

Kania's congress speeches were rigidly centrist and full of praise for the USSR and its foreign policy. The new party statute provided for secret elections and at most two five-year terms for all party officials.

The congress restored some of the party's morale and at least a little of its authority. It also showed how much the overwhelming majority of the party wanted a return to peace and order. Yet it adopted no clear program and although its procedures were democratic, its results were so politically balanced that it did not mark a final victory for either reform or reaction. Moreover, the new central committee was politically inexperienced and therefore unlikely to be as much of a control organ over the apparat as it was pledged to be. Furthermore, although the center was strengthened, the hard-liners and the reformers were still represented in the politburo. Thus the struggle for power— and for policies—would continue.

Poland's economic problems continued to get worse. As Jaruzelski said at the congress, net income declined 15 percent and wages rose 23 percent from January through June, foreign debt was expected to rise $3 billion more, the supply of goods available was 10 percent less, and prices would have to be raised 110 percent to take up the slack. Moreover, new strike threats loomed, including LOT, the national airline, whose workers, in what might become a test of Solidarity's aim to have firms controlled by their workers, demanded that they be allowed to choose their own director, and the government refused.

The USSR

By mid-1981 the Soviets had not intervened militarily in Poland, although they had twice come extremely close—perhaps only by hours—to doing so in the first week in December 1980 and again in the first week in April 1981. Both times Brezhnev had decided to postpone his decision. Whether or not it would stay postponed remained unclear. They were, and realized that they were, damned if they did and damned if they did not.

The Soviets underestimated the speed and extent of Polish developments. They procrastinated. They tried to strengthen the Polish Communist party by constantly threatening intervention and by giving Poland a $1.3 billion credit, $1.1 billion in hard currency. They twice unsuccessfully tried to replace the Polish communist leadership with pro-Soviet hard-liners. By mid-1981, however, they had had considerable impact on developments in Poland, and invasion, although at least postponed, seemed no longer imminent. (In response to repeated intensifying Western warnings of the dire consequences of an invasion of Poland, Moscow always replied that it had no such intention.)

The costs to Moscow of invading and of not invading Poland were far more serious than with Hungary in 1956 and Czechoslovakia in 1968. For example, Poland has always been the principal invasion route into the USSR from the West. Since 1945 it has divided the USSR from East Germany, control over which is essential for Moscow to maintain, as it is determined to do, a divided and weak Germany. Second, in Hungary and Czechoslovakia the initiative had come from within the party and the intelligentsia, but in Poland in 1980 it was a spontaneous workers' movement, the worst menace to any Leninist. (Remember Lenin's and Trotsky's ruthless crushing of the Kronstadt rebellion.) Third, Poland has historically always been strongly anti-Soviet and pro-Western. A free Poland was therefore the more dangerous to the USSR and the more necessary to maintain under firm Soviet control. Fourth, the USSR also had so many other problems—notably, with Afghanistan, LRTNF deployment, the new Reagan administration, and Chinese-sponsored encirclement—that it in theory cannot afford to allow the Polish developments to continue and consolidate. Think, after all, of the effect of such developments in East Germany, Czechoslovakia, the Baltic states,[34] and the Ukraine. The more and the longer the Polish workers hold on to their gains, the more, probably, they will gradually infect the rest of Eastern Europe, beginning with its developed parts and eventually, perhaps, the non–Great Russian parts of the USSR as well. How, when, where, and how much these gains will have an effect we cannot know. Fifth, the destabilization of Poland that has already occurred, to say nothing of what seems likely to come, has potentially endangered the Red Army's main line of communications with its twenty-two divisions in East Germany. Sixth, it seemed likely to open Poland up more and more to Western influence and to make it more and more difficult to enforce any effective media censorship there, including that of anti-Soviet material. Finally, while Khrushchev and Brezhnev had largely depoliticized the Soviet intelligentsia and crushed the dissident movements, the decline in Soviet economic growth made workers' unrest likely in the USSR later in the 1980s, and what happened in Poland might well stimulate it further.

However, the arguments against invasion were also very strong. First, the Soviets have long memories—for example, of the Polish sacking of Moscow in the early seventeenth century, of how the Poles fought when the tsars crushed the Polish risings of 1830 and 1963, and when the Nazis, with the Red Army standing by across the Vistula, crushed the Warsaw risings of 1944. Most Soviets, therefore, believed that if the Red Army invaded Poland, most of the Poles would fight, long and fiercely. The result would thus be to make the Red Army's lines of communication to East Germany, at least by rail, even more unreliable for at least some time. At first, therefore, a Soviet invasion force of perhaps around one million troops would be necessary. Second, the Polish party leadership, unlike Nagy and Dubček, were not revisionists. Solidarity were heathens, not heretics, and the Soviets, like other religions, have always found the former less dangerous than the latter. The Polish Communist party leadership was not searching for independence from the USSR; without the threat of Soviet intervention they could not keep themselves in power. Some, perhaps much, of the Polish army would probably fight. There would be a nationwide sit-down general strike and at least for some time thereafter an underground resistance movement that would require a long-term Soviet-troop commitment. Any East European units the Soviets used would not be very reliable, and if East German troops were used, they would only further enrage the Poles.[35] Third, Moscow would have to assume the Polish debt to the West (some $25 billion) and subsidize the Polish economy much more than it had already done. Fourth, invasion would threaten all Moscow's gains in Western Europe, end détente and Bonn's *Ostpolitik* there, drive the PCI and PCE to break completely with the CPSU, guarantee U.S.-LRTNF deployment in West Germany, and at least for a time reconsolidate U.S.–West European relations, thus ending, or at least postponing, Moscow's hopes to profit from their differences. (That an invasion might in fact eventually worsen the relations was also possible, but the Soviets would be taking a risk to assume this.) Fifth, the Red Army was fighting in Afghanistan and was heavily committed on the Chinese frontier. Finally, an invasion would probably play into the hands of the Chinese for it would intensify the encirclement of the USSR by driving Reagan closer to Beijing, cause Washington to arm China massively against the USSR, end all arms-control negotiations with the United States, and favor the superhawks over the hawks in Washington. The USSR had, in theory, other, intermediate alternatives: to try to have Warsaw declare martial law (but would the Polish army crush—or join—the general strike that it would surely provoke? Would this, indeed, not spark a Polish rising?); to conduct large-scale military maneuvers in Poland; or to change the Polish party leadership (but how and to what end, after it had so clearly failed to do so?). Or it could wait, as it had, hoping that Polish fervor would die down and that the Polish party leadership would again, as in 1956, 1970, and 1976, get the situation back under control. In mid-1981 Moscow seemed still to be waiting for that.

In mid-1981, the economic, and therefore political, challenge that faced Kania, Wałeça, and the church seemed likely to intensify. Could they keep the Polish working class quiet and persuade it to accept austerity in the face of its high expectations and declining standard of living? Would the party and Solidarity continue to compromise, especially on the key issue of workers' self-management, which Solidarity demanded and the party opposed? Or would confrontation become an explosive crisis?

7 The Crisis of the Western Alliance

Turkestan, Afghanistan, Transcaspia, Persia—to many these words breathe only a sense of utter remoteness, of a memory of strange vicissitudes and of moribund romance. To me, I confess, they are the pieces on a chessboard upon which is being played out a game for the domination of the world. —George Lord Curzon, Viceroy of India[1]

Andrer Bürger
Nichts Bessres weiss ich mir an Sonn- und Feiertagen
Als ein Gespräch von Krieg und Kriegsgeschrei,
Wenn hinten, weit, in der Türkei,
Die Völker auf einander schlagen.
Man steht am Fenster, trinkt sein Gläschen aus
Und sieht den Fluss hinab die bunten Schiffe gleiten;
Dann kehrt man abends froh nach Haus,
Und segnet Fried' und Friedenszeiten.

Dritter Bürger
Herr Nachbar, ja! so lass ich's auch geschehn,
Sie mögen sich die Köpfe spalten,
Mag alles durch einander gehn;
Doch nur zu Hause bleib's beim alten.

—Goethe *Faust* I. 860–871

In mid-1981, the West was in a more-serious, long-term crisis that at any time since the post-1945 reconstruction of Western Europe. It could agree neither on the nature and seriousness of the crisis nor on what new policies and institutions were needed to deal with it.

For the first time Western Europe and Japan were decisively, and the United States largely, dependent for energy on the Middle East, a non-Western, indeed largely anti-Western, region where instability was rising, the West was militarily weak, and the Iraqi-Iranian War threatened the security of energy supplies. The West was threatened and divided by Moscow's invasion of Afghanistan, the first post-1945 Soviet military move outside the Warsaw Pact area and one that improved Moscow's strategic position vis-à-vis the West in this region; by the Iraqi-Iranian War, which caused another oil price rise and further destabilized the West's economies including, for the first time, West Germany; and by the

Palestinian problem. The rise of the price of petroleum and the Western revolution of entitlements and lack of economic discipline had plunged the United States and its major allies, except West Germany and Japan, into endemic stagflation that interacted with and worsened the probably prolonged global economic crisis.

The new crisis was in part the result of Middle Eastern instability and Soviet expansionism. It was outside the NATO area, in a region where only the United States had major military power but where it was militarily inferior to the nearer Soviet forces. It thus challenged the NATO strategy of defense and détente. The Reagan administration gave priority to defense and Western Europe to détente.

The USSR tried to maintain control over its key security areas in Eastern Europe; to gain overwhelming nuclear and conventional military superiority in Europe; to lower the U.S. military presence in Western Europe, provided that it not be replaced by the West German Bundeswehr; to block the possibility of an anti-Soviet nuclear Germany; to prevent Western Europe from becoming united, militarily strong, and allied with China and the United States against it; and to play on the differences between the United States and Western Europe in order to move West Germany, by the carrot of allowing the continuation of arms control and *Ostpolitik* and the stick of harassment of *Ostpolitik* and rising Soviet power, into a mediating role between Moscow and Washington and thereafter down the slippery slope toward self-Finlandization and Soviet hegemony in Europe. Chancellor Schmidt, recently reelected, had no intention of playing this role, but many conservative Americans feared that he would be pushed into doing so.[2]

By 1981, the core of Western Europe was the close ties between France and the Federal Republic. The historic Franco-German enmity had largely disappeared. (Anglo-French rivalry had lasted much longer.) The French nuclear force and the French option to move away from Bonn toward Moscow balanced greater West German economic power. Britain, only half-heartedly European, continued to decline. Italy, whose situation seemed hopeless but not yet totally serious, remained pro–United States to avoid domination by the USSR, France, or West Germany as, to a lesser extent, did Benelux, Denmark, and Norway.

France and West Germany had special reasons to maintain détente with the USSR. France wanted to keep as much flexibility as possible in its foreign relations because a renewed cold war in Europe would again force it toward the United States, devalue it for the USSR as the West European state least dependent on the United States, thus menace it with a greater Soviet threat to its security, and lose its image in the world of its relative independence from the United States. The Federal Republic wanted to keep the security dividend and national gains of détente, the maintenance of the substance of the nation—that is, the travel of millions of West Germans to East Germany every year and the undisturbed security of West Berlin and its access routes from West Germany. However, for the first time, Washington and Bonn, not only Washington and Paris, were divided on key foreign policy issues.

The crisis in West European-U.S. relations had older, deeper causes, more elusive, more difficult to estimate, and more important. France and Germany saw the United States as powerful but jejune, a strange, alarming mixture of unpredictable changes, naive benevolence, canting hypocrisy, and ruthless materialism. To the West European cultural elites, much of U.S. society seemed to be a future to be feared, a plastic, consumerist mass culture. At least before, the United States had been strong and had saved them from Nazism. By the 1970s, however, France and the West Germany had again drifted apart from the United States. The postwar period of French and West German weakness and the common experience of the wartime generation on both sides of the Atlantic were over. Negative European perceptions of the United States revived.

For much of the French elite, the United States had become what they always thought it really was and for a growing proportion of the West German elite, what they reluctantly, sorrowfully came to accept that it had become: naive, weak, indecisive, spendthrift, increasingly ungovernable, vacillating between doing nothing in the face of the Soviet drive forward and trying recklessly and unilaterally to do too much too fast too soon. The two nations thought that the United States should not have fought the Vietnam War, should certainly not have lost it, and thereafter would not cut back inflation and energy imports. They were almost wholly dependent on Middle East petroleum, where they had little influence and therefore had to depend for its protection on the United States, whose Middle Eastern policies, they thought, were not only not determined by West European, but not even primarily by U.S. national interests, but rather by the U.S. pro-Israeli lobby. The United States, they thought, had reverted to provincialism, the result of the drift of its political epicenter away from the Northeast Establishment toward the South and the West, where neo-isolationism competed with machismo and the hot gospellers of degenerate Calvinism with plastic materialism. And their elites thought once again—as their fathers had, as Imperial Germany was convinced, and as France had always been certain—that only the continent had true culture and that the United States, like Great Britain, was only materialist. For many people on the continent, the United States was no longer an example to be imitated or a future to be hoped for but a present so dangerous because it could no longer lead the West. They therefore believed that they must try to restrain U.S. recklessness and compensate for U.S. weakness by preserving good relations with Moscow.

In France this was nothing new; it was part of the warp and woof of Gaullism. For Italy, the United States remained a more-desirable protector than France or Germany. The British still hoped to make up for their loss of economic and military power by their own cultural special relationship with the United States. The key new change was in the Federal Republic. Economically powerful and militarily vulnerable, twice the defeated enemy of the United States, and in 1981 still unavoidably dependent on it to contain Soviet power

—most of all around West Berlin—divided and nonnuclear by the consent of its allies as well as its enemies, the Federal Republic faced the most insoluble dilemma of all.[3]

Part of the West German problem was that most Americans had not yet realized the extent of its dilemma. Another part was that the United States had not yet adjusted to its own economic weakness and Bonn's economic strength. A third part was that after the 1979 invasion of Afghanistan, Washington suddenly reversed its policies toward the USSR after far too little consultation with Western Europe. The Americans were neither under any treaty obligation to defend West European interests in the Middle East, or even to consult with the West Europeans about it, for the Middle East and Southwest Asia were not covered by the NATO treaty, and CENTO and SEATO no longer existed.

Western Europe's dilemma was that it was an economic giant and a military dwarf. When the United States had been an economic giant as well, and before Western Europe had become one, West European dependence on Washington had been nearly total. Once it became an economic giant, Western Europe felt that it had the right to codetermine its own future. The United States, however, because of its new economic weakness, became less inclined to pay for defending the West European economic giant, the more so the West Europeans also expected the United States to provide the military defense for their energy interests, were unwilling to pay more for it, and were also unwilling, or at least very unenthusiastic, to support the sanctions that the United States (temporarily) tried to impose on the USSR after its invasion of Afghanistan.

An increasing group in the U.S. political elite thought Western Europe was weak and divided, prosperous and cynical; drifting into "Euroneutralism" because it was fearful of, and therefore appeased, Moscow; and keeping up a false pretense of cultural superiority, exceeded in its arrogance only by its expectation that the United States provide a free nuclear umbrella and troop presence to protect it while it profited from the trade with Moscow that the United States eschewed and from economic and monetary competition with the United States. Western Europe, they thought, sabotaged the U.S. attempt to contain Soviet power. Out of cynical thirst for Arab oil, it tried to sabotage the U.S.-sponsored Camp David process and thereby the U.S. determination to preserve the independence and security of Israel, whose establishment was the result of Nazi genocide and Anglo-French appeasement and which Western Europe was again ready to let be overrun.[4]

These West European-U.S. differences were still arched over by a continuing sense of the greater common threat—rising Soviet power and Middle Eastern instability—but they exacerbated specific policy differences. The most important one was about détente with the USSR. For West Europeans, détente had brought political stability and economic interdependence with the East. It had been at least partially institutionalized in CSCE and M(B)FR. Paris and Bonn were therefore determined to preserve Europe as an island of détente in

the midst of the second Soviet–U.S. cold war, this time in the Third World. However, most of the Reagan administration was determined to stop the USSR in the
Third World even if it risked the end of détente in Europe.

Ostpolitik thus again became a significant issue in Bonn's relations with the
United States because many people in Reagan's Washington had come to share
Kissinger's early doubts about it, and Schmidt, despite his determination not to
fight with him as he had with Carter, distrusted Reagan's distaste for détente.
Closer ties with, and economic and cultural influence on, East Germany had become vital West German national interests, not just SPD policies. West German
industry was determined to trade with the USSR and Eastern Europe. Low West
German economic growth made this trade more important. Bonn, like Paris, felt
that the West should give priority to improving relations with the Islamic countries, while Washington thought a greater Western military presence was more
productive and was unwilling to move decisively toward Islamic views on the
Palestinian issue. Finally, rising West German self-confidence made automatic
support of U.S. policies less likely in any case, and West German public opinion
had not been nearly as politicized, in an anti-Soviet direction, as U.S. public
opinion by the Americans held hostage in Iran.

In early 1981, Giscard was more fearful than Washington of *Ostpolitik's*
implications. He was also anxious to demonstrate his hard line against Moscow to lessen the danger from his Right. He therefore seemed to want to
improve his relations with Washington, with which he shared a common
concern about Bonn's *Ostpolitik*. His successor Mitterand intensified this
tendency.

These French and West German policies were national ones, shared by Right
and Left. They stabilized Western Europe and might even destabilize Eastern
Europe—just the reverse of Moscow's intention. Also, the French and West
Germans believed, they helped keep the Red Army out of Warsaw and thus preserved the gains of détente in Poland and Hungary. The U.S. political elite,
however, saw them as instruments with which the USSR blocked Paris and Bonn
from following the U.S. lead to preserve alliance security and energy supplies.
Ironically, the Franco-German alliance and the increasing effectiveness of the
foreign policy coordination of the nine EEC states, which by mid-1981 Mitter-
and seemed anxious to intensify, created some of the West European unity that
Washington had so long urged but that by 1981 so often found inconvenient.

Three other developments, one economic and the other two military, caused
U.S.–West European differences. They were doubly asymmetrical: economic to
the advantage of Western Europe and military-technological to the advantage of
the United States. The economic asymmetry arose, despite the recovery of the
dollar from the U.S. stagflation, in contrast to Continental European (and
Japanese) prosperity. Indeed, the deutsche–mark-dominated snake, one key
instrument of Franco-German leadership of Western Europe, was in part designed
to insulate the core of Western Europe from the vagaries and decline of the

dollar. Militarily, Western Europe was at a double disadvantage because the cost of new weapons systems was spiraling and advanced military technology required a continental base and had been developed in the United States. Finally, the pro-Palestinian West European stance antagonized Israel and deprived Western Europe of any influence over it, and increased differences between the United States and Western Europe about the Middle East. Since, with the partial exception of France, the West European governments had few if any cards to play in the Middle East, in theory their best bet would have been to try to influence the U.S. Middle Eastern policy. Yet their moving toward the PLO intensified the hostility to them in the United States.

* * *

Western Europe was a prisoner of a past that was dead and a future that was powerless to be born. It wanted to be no longer dependent on the United States. Yet militarily it was and could not soon be otherwise. It feared the USSR more than ever and tried in part to ensure its security and to limit its dependence on Washington by negotiating with Moscow. For both reasons it was unwilling to try to balance between China and the USSR, to say nothing of allying with Beijing, Washington, and Tokyo against Moscow.

France and West Germany were likely to continue to play the complex game we have discussed. Moscow, for its own purposes, would try to encourage them to do so, although if it were to invade Poland they would at least temporarily stop playing it. Washington would try, perhaps with diminishing success, to get Western Europe to follow its lead in putting pressure on Moscow.

Some Policy Considerations

How might the West, and particularly the United States, reverse the trend toward the decline of the Western alliance? Two of the main issues were financial and therefore very difficult to compromise: (1) East-West trade and (2) increases in defense expenditures. (The third was LRTNF deployment, which Moscow continued to try to block.) U.S. policies on both financial issues were quite different from West European ones—namely, Washington favored less East-West trade and higher defense expenditures than the West European states. This divergence was accentuated by the Soviet invasion of Afghanistan and caused by different traditions and threat perceptions. West Europeans never wanted to use East-West trade to punish the Soviets, and West European public opinion was far less willing than U.S. to increase defense expenditures. The United States saw the Soviet invasion of Afghanistan as a clear and present military danger to

Western security, but Paris and Bonn saw it as a primarily political problem that kept Moscow busy far from Europe. The Reagan administration took a stronger line than its predecessor toward the USSR. It thus seemed likely that West European–U.S. substantive differences would increase.

The Reagan administration declared that it wanted to improve relations with Western Europe (but then, so did all new U.S. administrations). Given their common conservatism and concern about the Soviet threat, it seemed likely that improved relations would indeed occur with London and Paris. However, indecision and internal feuding characterized the Reagan administration almost as much as its predecessor's. Substantive U.S.-West European differences were likely to become greater for Reagan took a much harder line vis-à-vis Moscow than Carter had, greatly increased the U.S. defense budget, pressed the West Europeans to do likewise, and did not move closer to the West European position on the Palestinian issue.

These differences were likely to be the most serious between Washington and Bonn. In Bonn, a center-left government was in power. The SPD left wing was questioning the LRTNF-deployment decision. The SPD and the Socialist International, of which Brandt was the chairman, supported the political arm of the guerrillas in El Salvador (as did Mitterand) while the Reagan administration was stepping up arms aid to the government there. And Bonn seemed determined to maintain its trade with the East.

The nostalgia in Western Europe was for détente; in the United States, predominance. However, a greater common sense of danger from the USSR did exist by early 1981, no matter how different the remedies for it were on different sides of the Atlantic. The Reagan administration seemed more anxious to consult with the West Europeans and less likely to blow an uncertain trumpet —however little the West Europeans might agree with some of its trumpeting. President Reagan and Secretary of State Haig seemed less likely than before to be seen by the West Europeans to be plotting double hegemony with Moscow. Thus, in sum, in early 1981 greater differences in substance were coupled with improvements in style.

The best method would be to set up new institutions to understand and cope with the crisis. The economic summits, which included Japan, did not deal with political and military problems. The political summits had not included Japan. What was needed was the equivalent of the foreign policy coordination of the nine states of the EEC—namely, regular, institutionalized meetings—initially about the Middle East—among the United States, France, West Germany, Great Britain, and Japan, frequent at senior levels, less frequent at the level of foreign ministers, and occasionally at the summit. The smallest possible joint secretariat should prepare the agenda, rotate the meetingplace, and write up the agreed results. A working group should initially define the nature of the alliance crisis and propose the institutions required to handle it and the policies to do so.[5]

This meant that on European problems, where Japanese interests are clearly not involved, the United States should regularly consult with the mechanism of European political cooperation within the limits of the latter's competence. It would not be easy for Washington. It would always seem easier to consult bilaterally with the French, or the West Germans, or the British, or two or three. It would also seem particularly irrelevant in Washington to consult with this mechanism when one of the smaller West European countries was in the chair. Yet in the longer-range U.S. interest, it should, but probably will not soon, be done.

As in the EEC, the states in this larger grouping would remain independent. Deferring to each other's interests would be far from easy, especially for the United States and France and above all in the Middle East. Agreements to disagree would often have to be settled for, but division of labor is not only the least common denominator but often a very desirable one. For example, the French might effectively intervene, as they did in Shaba II, to cope with local and regional instability, while the United States would often take the lead against Soviet movements of forces into Third World countries. The West Europeans could be helpful with the anti–Camp David Arabs, while only the United States could effectively influence or pressure Israel. Above all, only in such institutions could there develop the mutual trust that defuses looming alliance crises by telephone before they are pushed up to the summit and thence inevitably into the press.

The crucial points are three. First, a consultative mechanism for problems in the Third World must be set up as outlined here. Second, the United States must be prepared to make NATO a real alliance not, as it has been, an instrument for U.S. predominance over Western Europe. Third, the West Europeans must begin to negotiate with the United States as a unit for otherwise they will continue to be divided and frustrated.

U.S. foreign policy after World War II realized the necessity, in its national interest, that Western Europe unite. In the 1980s, few U.S. statesmen were left who were present at the creation, but in 1981 the recreation of Western unity was more urgent than ever. Such unity, not the cold war, détente, nor Soviet-U.S. double hegemony, remained the best guarantee of its security.

Endnotes

Chapter 1

1. Seweryn Bialer, *Stalin's Successors* (New York: Cambridge University Press, 1980); William E. Griffith, ed., *The Soviet Empire: Expansionism and Détente* (Lexington, Mass.: Lexington Books, D.C. Heath and Company, 1976); Stephen F. Cohen et al., eds., *The Soviet Union since Stalin* (Bloomington: Indiana University Press, 1980); Murray Feshbach, "A Different Crisis," *The Wilson Quarterly* (Winter 1981); George Feifer, "Russian Disorders," *Harper's* (February 1981); and Adam Ulam, *Expansion and Coexistence*, 2d ed. (New York: Praeger, 1974).

2. Zdeněk Mlynář, *Nightfrost in Prague* (New York: Karz, 1980), p. 240.

3. See the chapter by my colleague, Walter Dean Burnham, in Thomas Ferguson and Joel Rogers, ed., *Behind the Election* (New York: Pantheon, 1981); and Burnham, "Ronald Reagan's New Era" (unpublished ms., 1981).

4. Peter Steinfels, *The Neo-Conservatives* (New York: Simon and Schuster, 1979); Dennis H. Wrong, "The Rises and Fall (?) of the Neoconservatives," *Partisan Review*, no. 1 (1981); a symposium with Nathan Glazer, James Q. Wilson, Peter Steinfels, and Norman Birnbaum in *Partisan Review*, no. 4 (1980); James Q. Wilson, "Reagan and the Republican Revival," *Commentary* (October 1980); Daniel Bell, *The Cultural Contradictions of Capitalism* (New York: Basic, 1976); Bell, *The Winding Passage: Essays and Sociological Journeys 1960–1980* (Cambridge, Mass.: ABT, 1980); and Norman Podhoretz, *Breaking Ranks* (New York: Harper and Row, 1980).

5. What follows is largely drawn from Daniel Yankelovich and Larry Kaagan, "Assertive America," *Foreign Affairs* 39, no. 3 (1981) ("America and the World 1980").

6. William A. Watts and Lloyd A. Free, "Nationalism, Not Isolationism," *Foreign Policy* (Fall 1976); and John E. Rielly, "The American Mood: A Foreign Policy of Self-Interest," *Foreign Policy* (Spring 1979).

7. The beginning of this part is a revised version of William E. Griffith, "1980: A Year of Crises," MIT/CIS C-80/9, mimeographed, November 1980. It is in part based on conversations in Moscow in June 1980 and in April and June 1981, in Beijing in July 1979, and at the Sino-American Conferences on International Affairs, Washington, D.C., September 1979 and in Beijing, June 1981.

8. William G. Hyland, "The Sino-Soviet Conflict: A Search for New Security Strategies," in Richard H. Solomon, ed., *Asian Security in the 1980s: Problems and Policies for a Time of Transition*, RAND R-2492-ISA, 1979.

9. Dimitri Simes, "The Death of Détente," *International Security* (Summer 1980); Robert Legvold, "Containment without Confrontation," *Foreign*

Policy (Fall 1980); and Paul H. Nitze, "Strategy in the 1980s," *Foreign Affairs* (Fall 1980).

10. L.I. Brezhnev, "Za ukreplenie splochennosti kommunistov, za noboi pod' 'em anti-imperialistichekoi bor'by," *Pravda*, 8 June 1969, p. 4, quoted from Samuel B. Payne, Jr., *The Soviet Union and SALT* (Cambridge, Mass.: MIT Press, 1980), p. 96.

11. L.I. Brezhnev, "Na zemie ratnoi i trudovoi slavy," *Pravda*, 15 April 1970, p. 2, quoted from Payne, *The Soviet Union*, p. 97.

12. See the detailed and excellent analysis in Payne, *The Soviet Union*, pp. 29–62, 98–102.

13. Dimitri Simes, "Deterrence and Coercion in Soviet Policy," *International Security* (Winter 1980–1981).

14. Quoted from Pierre Hassner, "Europe: Old Conflicts, New Rules," *Orbis* (Fall 1973), p. 897 and tr. from Hassner, "L'Europe de la guerre froide à la paix chaude," *Défense nationale* (March 1973), pp. 45–47.

15. William E. Griffith, *The Ostpolitik of the Federal Republic of Germany* (Cambridge, Mass.: MIT Press, 1978), pp. 71–72.

16. William E. Griffith, *The Sino-Soviet Rift* (Cambridge, Mass.: MIT Press, 1964), p. 18.

17. Thomas M. Gottlieb, *Chinese Foreign Policy Factionalism and the Origins of the Strategic Triangle*, RAND R-1902-NA, November 1972; and Kenneth G. Lieberthal, *Sino-Soviet Conflict in the 1970s: Its Evolution and Implications for the Strategic Triangle*, RAND R-2342-NA, July 1978. For Sino-Soviet relations in the 1970s, see Herbert J. Ellison, ed., *The Sino-Soviet Conflict* (Seattle: University of Washington Press, 1981).

18. Quoted from Jerome H. Kahan, *Security in the Nuclear Age* (Washington, D.C.: Brookings Institution, 1975), pp. 110–113.

19. In an interview with *U.S. World and News Report*, 12 April 1965, p. 52, quoted from Albert Wohlstetter, "Is There a Strategic Arms Race?," *Foreign Policy* (Summer 1974), p. 18. I owe these first two quotations to Payne, *The Soviet Union*.

20. Leslie H. Gelb, "A Glass Half Full," *Foreign Policy* (Fall 1979), p. 21.

21. I have profited from comments on an earlier draft of this part by William Kaufmann, Michael Nacht, Jack Ruina, Kosta Tsipas, and John Van Oudenaren.

22. In my view, the ablest presentation of the case against the ratification of SALT II is Uwe Nerlich, "Die Rüstungskontrollwirkungen des SALT-II Abkommens," Stiftung Wissenchaft und Politik SWP-AP 2226, July 1979. See also his "Theatre Nuclear Forces in Europe," *Washington Quarterly* (Winter 1980); and the articles by John Lehman (appointed by President Reagan as secretary of the navy) and Henry Rowan in the SALT symposium in the *Washington Quarterly* (Winter 1979).

23. Johan J. Holst and Uwe Nerlich, eds., *Beyond Nuclear Deterrence* (New York: Crane Russak, 1977); Richard Burt, *New Weapons Technologies,* Adelphi Paper no. 126 (London: IISS, Summer 1976); Burt, "Technology and East-West Arms Control," *International Affairs* (January 1977); James F. Digby, *Precision Guided Weapons,* Adelphi Paper no. 118 (London: IISS, Summer 1975); Kosta Tsipas, "Cruise Missiles," *Scientific American* (February 1977); William Kincade, "Over the Technological Horizon," *Daedalus* (Winter 1981); and Donald M. Snow, "Lasers, Charged-Particle Beams, and the Strategic Future," *Political Science Quarterly* (Summer 1980).

24. For analyses of Soviet nuclear-doctrine thinking, see three articles that emphasize its asymmetry with U.S. doctrine: Benjamin S. Lambeth, "The Political Potential of Soviet Equivalence," *International Security* (Fall 1979); Fritz W. Ermarth, "Contrasts in American and Soviet Strategic Thinking," *International Security* (Fall 1978); and Daniel Patrick Moynihan, "Reflections: The SALT Process," *New Yorker,* 19 November 1979; and two other articles that see more congruence: Raymond L. Garthoff, "Mutual Deterrence and Strategic Arms Limitation in Soviet Policy," *International Security* (Summer 1978) [and a rejoinder by Donald Brennan in *International Security* (Winter 1978-1979)]; and Robert Legvold, "Strategic 'Doctrine' and SALT: Soviet and American Views," *Survival* (January–February 1979). For emphasis on Soviet adherence to a nuclear-war-fighting capability, see Richard Pipes, "Why the Soviet Union Thinks It Could Fight and Win a Nuclear War," *Commentary* (July 1977); and Joseph D. Douglass, Jr., and Amoretta M. Hoeber, *Soviet Strategy for Nuclear War* (Stanford, Calif.: Hoover Institution, 1979).

25. The phrase is Benjamin Lambeth's.

26. Lambeth, "Political Potential of Soviet Equivalence," p. 25.

27. A.A. Gromyko, "The Peace Program in Action," *Kommunist,* no. 14 (September 1975): 5, quoted from Lambeth, "Political Potential of Soviet Equivalence," p. 33.

28. Moynihan, "Reflections: The SALT Process," p. 121.

29. Richard Burt, "Reassessing the Strategic Balance," *International Security* (Summer 1980); and Burt, "Toward a New Balance in Defense and Arms Control Policies," in Uwe Nerlich, ed., *Military Force and Negotiation* (forthcoming). See also Burt, "Washington and the Atlantic Alliance: The Hidden Crisis," in W. Scott Thompson, ed., *From Weakness to Strength* (San Francisco: Institute for Contemporary Studies, 1980.) This volume provides a convenient collection of views by various conservative strategies, many of whom have become prominent in the Reagan administration (Burt, for example, became director of politico-military affairs in the Department of State). See also Albert Wohlstetter, "Racing Forward or Ambling Back?," and Paul H. Nitze, "Nuclear Strategy: Détente and American Survival," in Institute of Contemporary Studies, ed., *Defending America* (New York: Basic, 1977), an earlier

volume setting forth similar views, and for a very sophisticated pro-BMD position, see Colin S. Gray, "A New Debate on Ballistic Missile Defense," *Survival* (March-April 1981).

30. Escalation dominance refers to a sufficient force to escalate as one wishes while deterring one's opponent from doing the same.

31. Arms controllers maintained that there might be serious questions about whether this could be done effectively with existing technology.

32. Primarily by the National Security Council and the Department of Defense with the State Department generally opposed.

33. PD 41, "U.S. Civil Defense Policy," 29 September 1978, declassified 23 June 1980.

34. I draw here on the remarks of Philip Windsor of the London School of Economics at the European-American Conference on Negotiated Constraints in Europe, 11–13 June 1980, at Ebenhausen/Obb.; see the summary in Stiftung Wissenschaft und Politik, SWP-AP 2257, July 1980, p. 11. The conference presentations will be published in a book edited by Uwe Nerlich, *Military Force and Negotiation.*

35. Nerlich, "Change in Europe: A Secular Trend?," *Daedalus,* (Winter 1981).

Chapter 2

1. See Joseph D. Douglass, Jr., *Soviet Military Strategy in Europe* (New York: Pergamon, 1980), which stresses the Soviet expectation that a war in Europe will rapidly become nuclear.

2. John Van Oudenaren, "The Soviet Conception of Europe and Arms Control," in Uwe Nerlich, ed., *Military Force and Negotiation* (forthcoming); Van Oudenaren, "The Leninist Peace Policy and Western Europe," MIT/CIS C/80-1, mimeographed, January 1980; Hannes Adomeit, "The Soviet Union and Western Europe," National Security Series no. 3/79, Centre for International Relations, Queens University, Kingston, Ontario; Robert Legvold, "The Soviet Union and Western Europe," in William E. Griffith, ed., *The Soviet Empire: Expansion and Détente* (Lexington, Mass.: Lexington Books, D.C. Heath and Company, 1976); and Uwe Nerlich, "Change in Europe: A Secular Trend?," *Daedalus* (Winter 1981).

3. Rudolf Bahro, *The Alternative in Eastern Europe* (London: New Left Books, 1978.) For a very sympathetic analysis, see David Bathrick, "A Paradigm for Dissent: Rudolf Bahro's Alternative" (Paper delivered at the New England Slavic Conference, April 1978.)

4. For East Germany in the 1970s, see Hartmut Zimmerman, "The GDR in the 1970s," a long, detailed, and authoritative analysis; William Treharne Jones, "East German Literature," and Stephen R. Bowers, "Youth Policies in the GDR," *Problems of Communism* (March-April 1978).

5. William E. Griffith, "The West German–American Relationship: The Threat of Deterioration," *Washington Quarterly* (Summer 1979); Marion Dönhoff, "Bonn and Washington: The Strained Relations," *Foreign Affairs* (Summer 1979); Alex A. Vardamis, "German-American Military Fissures," *Foreign Policy* (Spring 1979); and W.R. Smyser, *German-American Relations*, Washington Papers no. 74 (Beverly Hills and London: Sage, 1980).

6. Fritz Stern, "Germany in a Semi-Gaullist Europe," *Foreign Affairs* (Spring 1980).

7. See the penetrating discussion by Christoph Bertram, "European Security and the German Problem," *International Security* (Winter 1979–1980), which in my view, underestimated the continuing pull of the issue of reunification.

8. Text of his interview with the Deutschlandfunk, 23 March 1980, in *Informationen der Sozialdemokratischen Bundestagsfraktion*, no. 286 (23 March 1980).

9. *Frankfurter Allgemeine Zeitung*, 17 and 18 March 1980.

10. *Frankfurter Allgemeine Zeitung*, 24 March 1980.

11. Conversations in Bonn and Berlin, March and June 1980. See also the remarkable reprinting of strong (if implicit) criticism of the Soviet invasion of Afghanistan by a high Yugoslav official on a state visit to East Berlin in *Neues Deutschland*, 14 February 1980.

12. *Frankfurter Allgemeine Zeitung*, 15 February 1980.

13. Stern. "Germany in a Semi-Gaullist Europe." See also Gregory F. Treverton, "Global Threats and Trans-Atlantic Allies," *International Security* (Fall 1980); and a comment by Klaus Mehnert in *The Washington Quarterly* (Winter 1981). The foreign policy of the new West German Protestant, pacifist, pietist movement was best set forth in the remarkable book by one of the ideologists of *Ostpolitik*, Peter Bender, *Das Ende des ideologischen Zeitalters. Die Europäisierung Europas* (West Berlin: Severin und Siedler, 1981). See also the manifesto of the wave's main figure, Erhard Eppler, *Wege aus der Gefahr* (Reinbek bei Hamburg: Rowohlt, 1981).

14. Conversations in Bonn, April-June 1981.

15. My treatment of *Ostpolitik* relies primarily on Griffith, *The Ostpolitik of the Federal Republic of Germany* (Cambridge, Mass.: MIT Press, 1978). I have also drawn on my updating of it for the German translation, *Die Ostpolitik der Bundesrepublik Deutschland* (Stuttgart: Klett-Cotta, 1981). For the most recent West German political developments, I have relied on a presentation by Guido Goldman at the Harvard Center for European Studies, 6 March 1981 and on conversations in West Germany, April-July 1981. For East Germany's doubling of travel costs and its background, see Peter Jochen Winters, "Kurswechsel Ost-Berlins gegenüber Bonn," *Europa Archiv*, 10 January 1981.

16. The most detailed and authoritative analysis of the CSCE at Helsinki and Geneva is John Maresca, *To Helsinki* (unpublished ms.). Mr. Maresca was a member of the U.S. delegation throughout the conference, ending as deputy

head. See also Luigi Vittorio Ferraris, ed., *Report on a Negotiation* (Alphen aan den Rijn: Sijhoff, 1980), tr. from *Testimonianze di un negoziato* (Padua: CEDAM, 1977), with extensive bibliography (Signor Ferraris was depty head of the Italian delegation); Karl Birnbaum, "East-West Diplomacy in the Era of Multilateral Negotiations: The Case of the Conference on Security and Coopera-tion in Europe (CSCE)," in Nils Andrén and Karl Birnbaum, eds., *Die Konferenz über Sicherheit und Zusammenarbeit in Europa: eine Zwischenbilanz der Genfer Kommissionsphase* (Bonn: Forschunginstitut der Deutschen Gesellschaft für Auswartige Politik, Arbeitspapiere zur Internationale Politik, no. 2, May 1974); Stephen J. Flannagan, "The CSCE and the Development of Détente," in Derek Leebaert, ed., *European Security: Prospects for the 1980s* (Lexington, Mass. Lexington Books, D.C. Heath and Company, 1979), pp. 189–232; Uwe Nerlich, "Zur Struktur und Dynamik europäischer Sicherheitspolitik," *Europa Archiv,* 25 July 1971; Paul Frank, "Zielsetzungen der Bundesrepublik Deutschland im Rahmen Europäischer Sicherheitsverhandlungen," *Europa Archiv,* 10 March 1972; Hans-Georg Wieck, "Überlegungen zur Sicherheit in Europa, *Aussenpolitik* (July 1972); Hans-Peter Schwarz, "Sicherheitskonferenz und westliche Sicher-heitsgemeinschaft," *Europa Archiv,* 25 December 1972; Guido Brunner, "Das Ergebnis von Helsinki," *Europa Archiv,* 10 July 1973; Götz von Groll, "East-West Talks in Helsinki," (*Aussenpolitik,* English ed.), no. 4 (1972); "The Foreign Ministers in Helsinki," *Aussenpolitik,* Eng. ed., no. 3 (1973); "The Geneva CSCE Negotiations," *Aussenpolitik,* Eng. ed., no. 2 (1974); "The Geneva Final Act of the CSCE," *Aussenpolitik,* Eng. ed., no. 3 (1975); Wolfgang Wagner, "Eine Station auf einem langen Wege. Zur geschichtlichen Einordnung der Konferenz über Sicherheit und Zusarmenarbeit in Europa (KSZE), *Europa Archiv,* 10 August 1975; Otto Graf Schwerin, "Die Solidaritat der EG-Staaten in der KSZE," *Europa Archiv,* 10 August 1975; Gerhard Henze, "Neue Aufgaben der Entspannungspolitik," *Europa Archiv,* 25 September 1975; Klaus Blech, "Die KSZE als Schritt im Entspannungsprozess," *Europa Archiv,* 25 November 1975; Leo Mates, "Europa nach der KSZE," *Europa Archiv,* 25 November 1976; Gregory A. Flynn, "The Content of European Détente," *Orbis* (Summer 1976); and Timothy W. Stanley and Darnell M. Whitt, *Détente Diplomacy: The United States and European Security in the 1970s* (New York: Dunellen, 1970).

For Soviet policy toward CSCE, see Marshall D. Shulman, "A European Security Conference," *Survival* (December 1969) Robert Legvold, "European Security Conference," *Survey* (Summer 1970); Boris Meissner, "The Soviet Union and Collective Security," *Aussenpolitik,* no. 3 (1970); Gerhard Wettig, "Soviet Shifts in European Security Policy," *Aussenpolitik* (English ed.), no. 3 (1970); Gerbard Wettig, "Gesamteuropäische kollektive Sicherheit und osteuropäische kollektive Souveranität als Elemente des sowjetischen Europa-Programs," *Berichte des Bundesinstituts für ostwissenschaftliche und inter-nationale Studien,* no. 25 (1972); Lilita Dzirkals and A. Ross Johnson, eds., *Soviet and East European Forecasts of European Security: Papers from the 1972*

Varna Conference, RAND R-1272-PR, June 1973; Ye. A. Boltin, *Sovetskaya Vneshnaya Politika i Europeiskaya Bezopasnost'* (Moscow, 1972), tr. in JPRS 87815, 20 December 1972; Charles Andras, "East-West Cooperation and Ideological Conflict," *Radio Free Europe Research,* 5 September 1973; Wettig, "Etappen der sowjetischen Europa-Politik im Blick auf KSZE und MBFR." *Berichte des Bundesinstituts für ostwissenschaftliche und internationale Studien,* no. 39 (1973); Wettig, "Sowjetische Vorstellungen über eine Neuordnung der zwischenstaatlichen Beziehungen in Europa," *Berichte des Bundesinstituts für ostwissenschaftliche und internationale Studien,* no. 40 (1974); Philippe Devillers, "La conférence sur la securité et la coopération en Europe," *Défense nationale,* no. 3 (1973); Mojmir Povolny, "The Soviet Union and the European Security Conference," *Orbis* (Spring 1974); Wettig, "Freiere Begegnungen und Dialoge zwischen Ost und West," *Aus Politik und Zeitgeschichte,* 15 March 1975; Andras, "European Security and 'Social Process,'" *Radio Free Europe Research,* 21 July 1975; Wettig, "Zum Ergebnis der KSZE," *Osteuropa* (December 1975); and Wettig, *Frieden und Sicherheit in Europa* (Stuttgart: 1975).

For East European attitudes, see Peter Bender, *East Europe in Search of Security* (London: Chatto and Windus, 1972); Robert R. King and Robert L. Dean, eds., *East European Perspectives on European Security and Cooperation* (New York: Praeger, 1974); John C. Campbell, "European Security: Prospects and Possibilities for East Europe," *East Europe* (November 1970); Robin Alison Remington, "Yugoslavia and European Security," *Orbis* (Spring 1973): Adam Bromke, "The CSCE and Eastern Europe," *The World Today* (May 1973).

For assessments of Soviet policy since Helsinki, see F. Stephen Larrabee, "Soviet Attitudes and Policy towards 'Basket Three' since Helsinki," *Radio Liberty Research,* 15 March 1976; Larrabee, "Soviet Implementation of the Helsinki Agreement: The Military Dimension," *Radio Liberty Research,* 1 January 1977; Ignacy Szenfeld, "Cooperation in the Field of Cultural Exchanges since the Helsinki Conference," *Radio Liberty Research,* 5 January 1977; Marshall Goldman, "Cooperation in the Field of Economics: The Soviet Side and Basket Two," *Radio Liberty Research,* 10 January 1977.

17. See the earlier analysis by a Yugoslav CSCE delegate, Ljubivoje Aćimović, "Die blockfreien Länder und die europäische Sicherheit," *Europa Archiv,* 10 December 1969.

18. See, in general, Curt Gasteyger, "Europa zwischen Helsinki und Belgrad," *Europa Archiv,* 10 January 1977.

19. By far the best analysis of the Belgrade conference, on which I have principally relied here, is Curt Gasteyger, "Die Aussichten der Entspannung Europa nach dem KSZE-Treffen in Belgrad," *Europa Archiv,* no. 15 (1978), reprinted in Hermann Volle and Wolfgang Wagner, eds., *Das Belgrader KSZE-Folgetreffen. Der Fortgang des Entspannungsprozesses in Europa in Beiträgen und Dokumenten aus dem Europa Archiv. Beiträgen und Dokumenten aus dem Europa Archiv* (Bonn: Verlag für internationale Politik, 1978), see also for other

analyses, notably by Aćimović, Per Fischer (the West German chief delegate), and Matthew Nimetz (a U.S. delegate). For the Soviet attitude, see Gerhard Wettig, "Die Warschauer-Pakt-Staaten auf der Belgrader Folgekonferenz," *Berichte des Bundesinstituts für ostwissenschaftliche und internationale Studien,* no. 15 (1978). For an excellent British analytical view, see Richard Davy, "No Progress at Belgrade," *The World Today,* (April 1978). For very critical views of Goldberg's activities, see Don Cook, "Making America Look Foolish. The Case of the Bungling Diplomat," *Saturday Review,* 13 May 1978; and Carroll Sherer (a U.S. delegate), "Breakdown at Belgrade," *Washington Quarterly* (Autumn 1978). For a favorable view of Goldberg, see "What the West Accomplished in Belgrade," *Business Week,* 30 January 1978. For three contemporary European analyses, see R. St., "Epilog zu Belgrad," *Neue Zürcher Zeitung,* 11 March 1978; Francois Fejtö, "Due lexioni da Belgrado," *Il Giornale,* 24 March 1978; and especially Gerhard Wettig, "Die sicherheitspolitischen Auseinandersetzungen auf der KSZE-Folgenkonferenz," *Berichte des Bundesinstituts für ostwissenschaftliche und internationale Studien,* no. 18 (May 1978), tr. as "Security Policy and CSCE in Belgrade," *Aussenpolitik* (English ed.) (Fall 1978).

20. As of mid-1981, the best overall coverage of the Madrid conference that I have seen, and on which this discussion was based, appeared in the *Frankfurter Allgemeine Zeitung,* the *Neue Zürcher Zeitung,* and *Economist.*

21. Markham from Madrid in *The New York Times,* 18 February 1981; Haubrich from Madrid in *Frankfurter Allgemeine Zeitung,* 8 and 21 July 1981.

22. Officially, "Mutual Reduction of Forces and Armaments and Associated Measures in Central Europe (MRFAAMCE). Moscow refused to accept "balanced," and the West insisted on the addition of "associated measures." By far the best, and most critical, analysis of M(B)FR in my view is Jeffrey Record, *Force Reductions in Europe: Starting Over* (Cambridge, Mass.: Institute for Foreign Policy Analysis, 1980). Another analysis is John G. Keliher, *The Negotiations on Mutual and Balanced Force Reductions* (New York: Pergamon, n.d. [1980]). See also William E. Griffith, "East-West Détente in Europe," in F.A.M. Alting von Geusau, ed., *Uncertain Détente* (Alphen aan den Rijn: Sijthoff and Noordhoff, 1979); Christoph Bertram, "European Arms Control," in Andrén and Birnbaum, *Beyond Détente;* Joseph I. Coffey, *Arms Control and European Security* (New York: Praeger, 1977), pp. 136–174; John Yochelson, "MBFR: The Search for an American Approach," *Orbis* (Spring 1973); Joseph I. Coffey, "Arms Control and the Military Balance in Europe," *Orbis* (Spring 1973); Alfons Pawelczyk, "Möglichkeiten eines Streitkräfte-Abbaus in Europa," *Europa Archiv,* 25 January 1977; Johan Jørgen Holst, "East-West Negotiations, Arms Control and West European Security," Norsk Utenrikspolitisk Institutt, Oslo, NUPI-N-91, April 1975; Jacques Huntzinger, "Les interrogations de Vienne," *Le Monde,* 20–21 June 1976 and 7 May 1976; Joseph I. Coffey, "Détente Arms Control and European Security," *International Affairs* (London) (January 1976); Gerhard Wettig, "Die sowjetische MBFR-Politik als Problem der Ost-West Entspannung in

Europa. *Berichte des Bundesinstituts für ostwissenschaftliche und internationale Studien*, no. 4 (December 1979); Christoph Bertram, "The Politics of MBFR," *The World Today* (January 1973); Bertram, *Mutual Force Reductions in Europe: The Political Aspects*, Adelphi Papers no. 84 (London: IISS, January 1972); Lother Ruehl, "Beiderseitige Truppenverminderung in Europa," *Europa Archiv*, 25 May 1973; Ruehl, "Die Wiener Verhandlungen über Truppenverminderung im Ost und West," *Europa Archiv*, 10 August 1974; Uwe Nerlich, "Die Rolle beiderseitiger Truppenverminderung in der europäischen Sicherheitspolitik," *Europa Archiv*, 10 March 1972; Nerlich, "Continuity and Change: The Political Context of Western Europe's Defense," in Johan Holst and Uwe Nerlich, eds., *Beyond Nuclear Deterrence* (New York: Crane, Russak, 1977); John Borawski, "Mutual Force Reduction in Europe from a Soviet Perspective," *Orbis* (Winter 1979); John Lehman, "Soviet Policy in Mutual and Balanced Force Reductions: Finlandization Denied," in George Ginsburgs and Alvin Z. Rubinstein, eds., *Soviet Foreign Policy toward Western Europe* (New York: Praeger, 1978), pp. 183–188; and John Erickson, "MBFR: Force Levels and Security Requirements," *Strategic Review* (Summer 1973). I also benefited from participation in a Harvard Program for Science and International Affairs Workshop on Force Restructuring and Force Reduction in Europe, November 1974, particularly from the papers by Steven L. Canby, Colin Gray, and General Andrew Goodpaster (for the Soviet position on MBFR); Yu. Kostko, "'The Balance of Fear' or the Safeguarding of Genuine Security," *Mirovaya ekonomika i mezhdunarodniye otnosheniya* (June 1972), tr. in *Survival* (September-October 1972); Coit Dennis Blacker and Farooq Hussain, "European Theater Nuclear Forces," *Bulletin of the Atomic Scientists* (October 1980); and for the lack of realism in collateral-damage computer models, see Paul Bracken, "On Theater Warfare," Hudson Institute HI-3036-P, 1 July 1979. See also John Erickson, "Soviet Theatre-Warfare Capability: Doctrines, Deployments and Objectives," mimeographed ms., Edinburgh, March 1975. For general background, see John Newhouse, *U.S. Troops in Europe* (Washington: D.C.: Brookings Institution, 1971; Robert Lucas Fischer, *Defending the Central Front: The Balance of Forces*, Adelphi Paper no. 127 (London: IISS, Autumn 1976); and *The Modernization of NATO's Long-Range Theater Nuclear Forces* (Report prepared for the Subcommittee on Europe and the Middle East of the Committee on Foreign Affairs, U.S. House of Representatives, 96th Cong., 2d Sess., Committee Print, by the Foreign Affairs and National Defense Division, Congressional Research Service, Library of Congress (Washington, D.C.: GPO, 1981).

The Soviets never accepted the phrase, "and balanced"; I have therefore put it in parentheses throughout.

23. C.G. Jacobsen, "Soviet Strategic Objectives for the 1980s"; and Anders C. Sjaastad, "Security Problems on the Northern Flank," *World Today*, (April 1979). See also Kenneth A. Myers, *North Atlantic Security: The Forgotten Flank?* and Edward N. Luttwak and Robert G. Weinland, *Sea Power in the*

Mediterranean: Political Utility and Military Constraints, Washington Papers no. 62 and 62, respectively (Beverly Hills and London: Sage, 1979).

24. Van Oudenaren, "Soviet Conception of Europe and Arms Control."

25. Richard Burt, *The New York Times,* 9 May 1979.

26. One report indicated that London and Bonn also had some bilateral discussions with Moscow on M(B)FR.

27. What follows draws largely on Record, *Force Reductions in Europe.*

28. Robert W. Dean, "Reposturing NATO's Long-Range Theater Nuclear Force: Examining the Case for New Deployments (unpublished RAND ms.); Gregory F. Treverton, "Nuclear Weapons and the 'Gray Area'," *Foreign Affairs* (Summer 1979); Treverton, "Long-Range Nuclear Weapons in Europe: The Choices" (Paper prepared for 4th Conference on New Approaches to Arms Control, Cumberland Lodge, Windsor Great Park, 16–18 May 1979); Uwe Nerlich, "Die landgestützte Stationierung von LRTNF und MX-Raketen: einige strategische und politische Zusammenhänge und Unterschiede," *Stiftung Wissenschaft und Politik* SWP-LN 2290, May 1981; Robert Metzger and Paul Doty, "Arms Control Enters the Gray Area," *International Security* (Winter 1978–1979); and Laurence Martin (in a symposium on SALT and U.S. policy) in the *Washington Quarterly* (Winter 1979); Christopher Makins, "Western Europe's Security; Fog over the 'Grey Areas'," *World Today* (February 1979); Johan J. Holst and Uwe Nerlich, eds., *Beyond Nuclear Deterrence,* esp. Burt, "Technological Change and Arms Control: The Cruise Missile Case" and Graham T. Allison and Frederic A. Morris, "Precision Guidance for NATO: Justification and Constraint"; Burt, *New Weapons Technologies,* Adelphi Papers no. 126 (London: IISS, Summer 1976); Burt, "Technology and East-West Arms Control," *International Affairs* (January 1977); Desmond Ball, "The Costs of the Cruise Missile," *Survival* (November-December 1978); Kosta Tsipas, "Cruise Missiles," *Scientific American* (February 1977); James F. Digby, *Precision Guided Weapons,* Adelphi Papers no. 118 (London: IISS, Summer 1975); Digby, "New Technology and Superpower Actions in Remote Contingencies," *Survival* (March-April 1979); Joseph I. Coffey, "Arms, Arms Control and Alliance Relationships: The Case of the Cruise Missile," mimeographed, University of Pittsburgh. For the SPD position, see SPD Parteivorstand, *Materialen* (for the November 1979 West Berlin SPD Parteitag), *Sicherheitspolitik. Leitantrag,* 9 September 1979. For Schmidt's position, see the interview with Hessischer Rundfunk, 14 October 1973, 0925 CMT (FBIS/WEUR/16 October 1979/J1); and Steven L. Canby, "Rethinking the NATO Military Problem," Wilson Center International Security Studies Program, Washington, D.C., Working Paper no. 3, mimeographed, June 1979. I also profited from a seminar on TNF and West German politics given by Professor Karl Kaiser at Harvard University on 17 December 1979. About the degree of military importance of Soviet SS-20 deployment, for the view that it has not to date changed current "something very close to parity," see *The Military Balance 1979–1980* (London: IISS, 1979), p. 117.

However, this same publication indicated that Soviet deployment above 250 SS-20s would occur and that the overall theater military balance was "moving steadily against the West" (p. 112). For criticism of the IISS argument, see a letter by Fred Charles Iklé in *The Economist* 10 November 1979 and K.-Peter Stratmann, "Das europäische Kräfteverhältnis," *Europa Archiv,* 10 July 1981. For an article by the IISS director in favor of LRTNF deployment, see Christoph Bertram, "Ringen um Raketen," *Die Zeit* (N. American ed.), 14 December 1979. I am grateful to Messrs. Digby, Tsipis, Jeffrey Boutwell (who is preparing a Ph.D. dissertation at MIT on LRTNF and West German domestic politics), John Van Oudenaren, and Professors John Deutch and W.W. Kaufmann for discussions on these matters.

For the military case against LRTNF deployment, see Kevin N. Lewis, "Intermediate-Range Nuclear Weapons," *Scientific American* (December 1980); for the political case from an arms-control viewpoint, see Klaas G. de Vries (of the Dutch Parliament), "Responding to the SS-20: An Alternative Approach," *Survival* (November-December 1979); Fred Kaplan, "Going Native without a Field Map," *Columbia Journalism Review* (January-February 1981); and Milton Leitenberg (of the Swedish Institute for International Affairs), "NATO and WTO Long Range Theatre Nuclear Forces," in Karl E. Birnbaum, ed., *Arms Control in Europe: Problems and Prospects* (Laxenburg, Austria: Austrian Institute for International Affairs, 1980). For the SS-21, SS-22, and SS-23, I have relied upon a seminar at the MIT Center for International Studies on 6 March 1981, given by Jack Keliher. See, for that and the West German political aspects, chapters by Keliher and Jeffrey Boutwell, respectively, in a forthcoming collective volume on TNF edited by Paul Doty of the Harvard Center for Science and International Affairs.

29. I have drawn heavily for this discussion on Uwe Nerlich, "Theatre Nuclear Forces in Europe," *Washington Quarterly* (Winter 1980).

30. Gerhard Wettig, "East-West Security Relations on the Eurostrategic Level," *Berichte des Bundesinstituts für ostwissenschaftliche und internationale Studien,* no. 27 (August 1980).

31. Jean-Louis Gergorin, "Les négotiations SALT et la défense de l'Europe," *Défense nationale* (June 1978); and Uwe Nerlich, "Die Rüstungskontrollwirkungen des SALT-II-Abkommens," *Stiftung Wissenschaft und Politik* SWP-AP 2226, July 1978.

32. See the penetrating and partly critical analysis by Lothar Ruehl, "Das Verhandlungsangebot der NATO an die Sowjetunion im Bereich der 'eurostrategischen' Waffen," *Europa Archiv,* 10 April 1980.

33. Kevin N. Lewis, "Intermediate-Range Nuclear Weapons," *Scientific American* (December 1980).

34. I have drawn extensively for this paragraph on Robert W. Dean, "Reposturing NATO's Long-Range Theater Nuclear Force: Examining the Case for New Deployments" (unpublished RAND ms.)

35. S.T. Cohen, *The Neutron Bomb: Political, Technological, and Military Issues* (Cambridge, Mass.: Institute for Foreign Policy Analysis, November 1978.)

36. The French proposal was for an all-European conference on conventional disarmament from the Atlantic to the Urals (CDE), thereby lessening the prospect of the two Germanies' being the major part of a MB(F)R special zone of disarmament, about which Bonn had always been worried, and leaving out French nuclear weapons. In 1981, this was still on the agenda of the Madrid CSCE follow-up meeting.

37. Text of his interview with the Deutschlandfunk, 23 March 1980, in *Informationen der Sozialdemokratischen Bundestagsfraktion,* no. 286, 23 March 1980. For the decline of the Bonn coalition's prestige in 1981, see Theo Sommer, "Nun doch Bitternis, Schweiss und Tränen," *Die Zeit,* 5 June 1981. For Brandt's trip to Moscow and an interview with him concerning it, see *Der Spiegel,* 6 July 1981.

38. *Pravda,* 7 October 1979.

39. Lothar Ruehl, "Moskau müsste seine Rakentenrüstung stoppen," *Die Zeit,* 13 June 1980.

Chapter 3

1. See David A. Deese and Joseph S. Nye, *Energy and Security* (Cambridge, Mass.: Ballinger, 1981), the most recent major study, with full bibliographies; the special issue of *Orbis* (Winter 1980) on energy and the Atlantic nations, especially the article by Hanns Maull; the summary by Achim von Heynitz and Friedemann Müller of an East-West workshop on energy at the Stiftung Wissenschaft und Politik, SWP-AP 2224, July 1979; Walter J. Levy, "But Dependence Will Continue," *Newsweek,* 1 June 1981.

2. I owe the point on automobiles to my colleague, Professor Alan Altshuler. For the decline in U.S. oil imports, see *Economist,* 28 February 1981, p. 16.

3. T. de Vries, "Saving the Dollar," *World Today* (January 1979); *OECD Economic Outlook,* no. 24 (December 1978): 6-7, 44-68; "New World Economic Order," *Business Week,* 24 July 1978; and "The Yankee Trader Is Back in Business," *Economist,* 9 December 1978. For the basic U.S. economic problems, see Lester Thurow, "The Moral Equivalent of Defeat," *Foreign Policy* (Spring 1981).

4. Harold van B. Cleveland and Ramachandia Bhagavatula, "The Continuing World Economic Crisis," *Foreign Affairs* 59, no. 3 (1981) ("America and the World 1980.")

5. Richard Portes, "East Europe's Debt to the West: Interdependence is a Two-Way Street," *Foreign Affairs* 55, no. 4 (July 1977): 751-782; Henry W.

Schaefer, "Energy and the Warsaw Pact. The Political Economy of Inter-dependence" (Paper prepared for the AAASS Meeting, Washington, D.C., 14-16 October 1977); "The CIA was half-right about oil," *The Economist,* June 6, 1981.

Chapter 4

1. Rudolf L. Tökés, *Dissent in the USSR* (Baltimore: Johns Hopkins University Press, 1975); and Robert Sharlet, "Growing Soviet Dissidence," *Current History* (October 1980).

2. Adam Ulam, *Russia's Failed Revolutions* (New York: Basic, 1981). For the view that the Soviet regime is stable, see Seweryn Bialer, *Stalin's Successors* (New York: Columbia University Press, 1980). For a more-sanguine view of Soviet dissidence, see Peter Reddaway, "The Development of Dissent in the USSR," in William E. Griffith, ed., *The Soviet Empire: Expansion and Détente* (Lexington, Mass.: Lexington Books, D.C. Heath and Company, 1976), pp. 57-84.

3. Rudolf L. Tökés, ed., *Opposition in Eastern Europe* (Baltimore: Johns Hopkins University Press, 1979); and a review article of recent books on the subject by Vlad Georgescu in *Problems of Communism* (July-August 1980). For Yugoslavia, see Dennison Rusinow, *The Yugoslav Experiment 1948-1974* (Berkeley and Los Angeles: University of California Press, 1977); the regular coverage by Slobodan Stanković in *Radio Free Europe Research;* and especially the analyses by Viktor Meier in the *Frankfurter Allgemeine Zeitung.* I am grateful to the latter two for long discussions over many years on Yugoslavia, most recently with Meier in Vienna in April 1981.

Chapter 5

1. See William E. Griffith, ed., *The European Left: Italy, France, and Spain* (Lexington, Mass.: Lexington Books, D.C. Heath and Company, 1979). For West European communism, see Rudolf L. Tökés, ed., *Eurocommunism and Détente* (New York: New York University Press for the Council on Foreign Relations, 1978); David Albright, ed., *Communism and Political Systems in Western Europe* (Boulder, Colo.: Westview, 1979); Vernon V. Aspaturian, Jiri Valenta, and David P. Burke, eds., *Eurocommunism between East and West* (Bloomington: Indiana University Press, 1980); Heinz Timmermann, "Reform-kommunisten in West und Ost," *Berichte des Bundesinstituts für ostwissen-schaftliche und internationale Studien,* no. 31, (September 1980); Wolfgang Leonhard, *Eurokommunismus; Herausforderung für Ost und West* (Munich: Bertelsmann, 1978); Annie Kriegel, *Un autre communisme?* (Paris: Hachette,

1977); Heinz Timmermann, ed., *Eurokommunismus* (Frankfurt: Fischer, 1978); and Donald L.M. Blackmer and Sidney Tarrow, eds., *Communism in Italy and France* (Princeton, N.J.: Princeton University Press, 1975). For Soviet policy toward West European communism, see Joan Barth Urban, "Moscow and the PCI in the 1970s: Kto Kovo?," *Studies in Comparative Communism* (Summer/ Autumn 1980) and her other articles cited therein; Heinz Timmermann, "Moskau und die Linke in Westeuropa," *Berichte des Bundesinstituts für ostwissenschaftliche und internationale Studien,* no. 12 (March 1980); Richard Lowenthal, "Moscow and the Eurocommunists," *Problems of Communism* (July–August 1978); Robert Legvold, "The Soviet Union and West European Communism," in Tökés, *Eurocommunism and Détente;* and William E. Griffith, "The Diplomacy of Eurocommunism," in Tökés, *Eurocommunism and Détente.* For running coverage, see the papers by Kevin Devlin in *Radio Free Europe Research* and Heinz Timmermann in *Berichte des Bundesinstituts für ostwissenschaftliche Studien.* For West European socialism, see Timmermann, "Democratic Socialists, Eurocommunists, and the West" in Griffith, *The European Left;* Timmerman, "Moskau und die Linke in Westeuropa"; the articles on West European socialism by Richard Lowenthal, Bogdan Denitch, and Jean-Pierre Worms in *Dissent* (Summer 1977); and Werner J. Feld, *The Foreign Policies of the West European Social Democratic Left* (New York: Praeger, 1978).

2. Peter Berton, "Japan: Euro-Nippo-Communism," in Aspaturian, ed., *Eurocommunism between East and West;* and David J. Myers, "Venezuela's MAS," *Problems of Communism* (September–October 1980).

3. I am grateful to Professor Peter Lange of Harvard University for discussions on these points.

4. See the analyses by Kevin Delvin in *Radio Free Europe Research,* 20 and 29 January 1981; Arnold Hottinger from Madrid in the *Neue Zürcher Zeitung,* 8 January 1981; and a forthcoming article by Eusebio Mujal-León in *Problems of Communism.*

5. For the resumption of PCI and PCE relations with the CCP, see *Beijing Review,* 28 April 1980; interview with Pajetta, *L'Unità,* 20 April 1980 (FBIS/ WEU/24 April 1980/L5); Reichlin, *L'Unità,* 20 April 1980 (FBIS/WEU/25 April 1980/L3). I have also benefited from discussions on this and other themes at a conference on European-U.S. relations in Rome, 25–28 May 1980, sponsored by the PCI and PSI research institutes and the Research Institute on International Change, Columbia University. For the PCE, see Kevin Devlin, "A Eurocommunist in Beijing: Carrillo's 'New Internationalism'," *Radio Free Europe Research,* 28 November 1980; and the various essays by Eusebio Mujal-León, including his chapters in the collective volumes edited by Tökés, Albright, and myself.

6. Kevin Devlin, "The French CP Enters its Seventh Decade," *Radio Free Europe Research,* 5 January 1981.

7. My analysis of the most recent developments profited greatly from a conference on the Eurocommunists' "new internationalism" at the Stiftung Wissenschaft und Politik, Ebenhausen/Obb., on 6–7 July 1981. See also Elizabeth Teague, "CPSU Spokesmen Criticize 'New Internationalism'," *Radio Liberty Research,* 1 July 1981.

8. For example, see Sidney Tarrow, "Italian Communism: The New and the Old," *Dissent* (Winter 1977); and Peter Lange and Maurizio Vannicelli, "Carter in the Italian Maze," *Foreign Policy* (Winter 1978–1979).

Chapter 6

1. From his classic study, *The Old Regime and the Revolution.*

2. This chapter is an expanded, revised, and updated version of William E. Griffith, "Poland Is Not Yet Lost" in Griffith, "1980: A Year of Crises," mimeographed, MIT/CIS, C/80-9, November 1980. As of mid-1981, the best overall analyses of recent Polish developements that I had seen were Seweryn Bialer, "Poland and the Soviet Imperium," *Foreign Affairs,* no. 3 (1981), "America and the World 1980;" Jan B. de Weydenthal, "Workers and Party in Poland," *Problems of Communism* (November–December 1980); Christoph Royen, "Der 'polnische Sommer' 1980. Zwischenbilanz und Ausblick." *Europa Archiv,* 25 December 1980 and "Polens Politisches System zwischen Beharrung und Erneurung," *Stiftung Wissenschaft und Politik,* SWP-AZ 2295, June 1981; Erik-Michael Bader, "Polens lange Krise," *Europa Archiv,* 25 February 1981; and Jiri Valenta, "Soviet Options in Poland," *Survival* (March–April 1981). The most interesting analyses by a Pole in a Western language that I have seen are three by a Polish sociologist who was imprisoned in 1968, taught in the Flying University, and became one of the experts at the Gdańsk August 1980 strike and who seems to me to write from a Western-Marxist viewpoint: Jadwiga Staniszkis, "On Remodelling of the Polish Economic System," *Soviet Studies* (October 1978); "On Some Contradictions of Socialist Society: The Case of Poland," *Soviet Studies* (April 1979); and especially "The Evolution of Forms of Working-Class Protest in Poland: Sociological Reflections on the Gdańsk-Szczecin Case, August 1980," *Soviet Studies* (April 1981). Dr. Staniszkis's book, *Dialectics of Socialist Society: The Case of Poland,* is to be published by the Princeton University Press. For background on recent developments, see Jan B. de Weydenthal, *Poland: Communism Adrift,* Wahsington Papers no. 72 (Beverly Hills and London: Sage, 1979); Abraham Brumberg, "The Open Political Struggle in Poland," *The New York Review of Books,* 8 February 1979; Brumberg, "The Revolt of the Workers," *Dissent* (Winter 1981); J.M. Montias, "Economic Conditions and Political Instability in Communist Countries: Observations on Strikes, Riots, and Other Disturbances," *Studies in Comparative Communism* (Winter 1980);

George Blazynski, *Flashpoint Poland* (New York: Pergamon, 1979), especially for the 1970 and 1976 strikes and the foundation of KOR; Peter Raina, *Political Opposition in Poland 1954-1977* (London: Poets and Painters Press, 1978), especially for the dissidence between 1956 and 1977 and for Kuroń and Michnik and the origins of KOR; Adam Michnik, *L'Église et la gauche* (Paris: Seuil, 1979), tr. from *Kościoł, Lewica, Dialog* (Paris: Institut Littéraire, 1977) especially for the rapprochement of Catholic and non-Catholic intellectuals; Zbigniew M. Fallenbuchel, "The Polish Economy at the Beginning of the 1980s," (the most authoritative analysis before the 1980 strikes) in U.S. Congress Joint Economic Committee, "Poland 1980: An East European Economic Country Study," 1 September 1980; Tadeusz Szafar, "Contemporary Political Opposition in Poland," *Survey* (Autumn 1979); Szafar, "The Political Opposition in Poland" (ms.); Jacques Rupnik, "Dissent in Poland 1968-1978: The End of Revisionism and the Rebirth of the Civil Society," in Rudolf Tökés, ed., *Opposition in Eastern Europe* (Baltimore: Johns Hopkins University Press, 1979); two special issues of *Survey* on Poland, Autumn 1979 and Winter 1980; Adam Przeworski, "Democratic Socialism in Poland?," (unpublished ms., October 1980); John Darnton (from Warsaw), "Sixty Days that Shook Poland," *The New York Times Magazine*, 9 November 1980; and Jule Gatter-Klenk, *Vielleicht auf Knien, aber vorwärts: Gespräche mit Lech Waleca* (Königstein/Taunus: Athenäum, 1981). The best running coverage from Warsaw has been by Bernard Guetta in *Le Monde* and by Bernard Margueritte in *Le Figaro;* see also Erik-Michael Bader in the *Frankfurter Allgemeine Zeitung,* Gert Baumgarten in the *Stuttgarter Zeitung,* Christopher Babinski in *Financial Times,* John Darnton in *The New York Times,* and Eric Bourne in the *Christian Science Monitor.* The best running analyses have been by J.B. de Weydenthal in *RFE Research.* "ok." [Bogdan Osadczuk-Korab] in the *Neue Zürcher Zeitung,* and in *The Economist.* For documentation, see Radio Free Europe, *The Pope in Poland* (Munich, 1979) and *August 1980: The Strikes in Poland* (Munich, 1980) and the documents and summaries in the books by Blazynski and Raina cited previously and in *Survey* (Autumn 1979 and Winter 1980). This chapter owes the most to my conversations during my three recent visits to Moscow and Warsaw in June 1980 and April and June 1981. I think it best, and I suspect that many of my conversation partners would agree, that I not acknowledge their assistance individually. I should, however, like to acknowledge the great help I have received from discussing Polish affairs over the years with Peter Bender, Seweryn Bialer, Zbigniew Brzezinski, Leo Labedz, John Michael Montias, Bogdan Osadczuk-Korab, William Schaufele, and Jan de Weydenthal.

    3. *August 1980: The Strikes in Poland.*

    4. Conversations in Warsaw, April and June, 1981.

    5. See the regular reviews of these publications in *RFE Research;* and Lidia Ciolkosz, "The Uncensored Press," *Survey* (Autumn 1979). See also the articles by Joseph Kay, Andrzej Szczpiorski, Andrzej Drawicz, and Tadeusz Szafar in *Survey* (Autumn 1979) and the extensive documentation therein.

6. For *Robotnik,* see *RFE Research,* Situation Report, Poland, 17/80, 17-18 September 1980, pp. 16-18 and *Survey* (Autumn 1979).

7. "How to Defend Ourselves," *Robotnik,* 30 May 1980, quoted from Brumberg, "The Revolt of the Workers," p. 26.

8. Jan B. de Weydenthal, "The Unofficial Report on Polish Politics and Society," *RFE Research,* 2 November 1979; and Weydenthal, "The Unofficial Program for Change in Poland," *RFE Research,* 2 July 1980. For its post-August 1980 views, see its draft program in *Avanti!,* 17 December 1980, analyzed in Kevin Devlin, "New Polish Reform Document Reported," *RFE Research,* 24 December 1980; and an article by its head, Stefan Bratkowski, in *Dissent* (Winter 1981) (originally in *Le Figaro,* 4 September 1980.)

9. Jacek Kuroń, "Reflections on a Program of Action," *Polish Review* (London), no. 3 (1977), quoted from Brumberg, "Revolt of the Workers," p. 25.

10. The best brief elaboration of this ideology in English translation, also a penetrating critique of the revisionists and the lay Catholics, was by Adam Michnik, "The New Evolutionism," *Survey* (Summer-Autumn 1976). For Michnik's biography, see Radio Free Europe, *August 1980,* pp. 334-335.

11. See the Writers' Union party cell bulletin, analyzed by Margueritte in *Le Figaro,* 4 August 1980.

12. Alexis de Tocqueville, *The Old Regime and the Revolution.*

13. The ablest analysis of the lessons of strikes and risings in Eastern Europe is J.M. Montias, "Economic Conditions and Political Instability." Except for the epilogue, it was written *before* the August 1980 strikes and was thus amazingly prophetic.

14. Guetta from Gdańsk, *Le Monde,* 19 August 1980.

15. See the penetrating DiP draft analysis in *Avanti!,* 17 December 1980, analyzed in Kevin Devlin, "New Polish Reform Document Reported," *RFE Research,* 24 December 1980.

16. *The Economist,* 1 November 1980, pp. 41-42; Jan B. de Weydenthal, "Poland's New Unions Gain a Place in the System," *RFE Research,* 20 November 1980.

17. Jan B. de Weydenthal, "Poland Asserts its Identity," *RFE Research,* 29 December 1980.

18. Darnton from Warsaw in *The New York Times,* 27 January 1981; Jan B. de Weydenthal, "The Problems of Power in Poland," *RFE Research,* 22 January 1981.

19. *Le Monde,* 20 February 1981.

20. *RFE Polish Situation Report,* 16 January 1981, pp. 16-22.

21. *RFE Polish Situation Report,* 3 October 1980, pp. 13-16. The union, Interim Committee of the Independent Agricultural Labor Unions (TKNZZR), was headed by Zdisław Ostatek, who had also been the head of the preparatory committee. For documentation, see *Survey* (Autumn 1979).

22. See the secret instructions of the Polish procurator-general in October 1980, in *The Times* (London), 27 November 1980; *Le Monde*, 29 November 1980; and *RFE Polish Situation Report*, 20 December 1980, pp. 13–20.

23. See the interview with Kuroń in *Der Spiegel*, 15 December 1980 (FBIS/EE/16 December 1980/G11–16); and Kuroń, "What Next in Poland?," *Dissent* (Winter 1981).

24. For example, concerning the limitation of the censorship, see the two draft laws, one by the ministry of justice and the other by a group of lawyers, journalists, and writers, in *Życie Warszawy*, no. 27 (1980) (FBIS/EE/5 December 1980/G 19–28.) For general party developments, see Jan B. de Weydenthal, "Party Attempts to Assert Itself Amid Threats of Soviet Intervention," *RFE Research*, 18 December 1980; and Bader in the *Frankfurter Allgemeine Zeitung*, 18 December 1980.

25. Bialer, "Poland and the Soviet Imperium"; and Cam Hudson, "Poland's Economy: November 1980," *RFE Research*, 13 November 1980.

26. Cam Hudson, "Polish Reformers Inspired by Hungarian Model," *RFE Research*, 22 January 1971.

27. A. Ross Johnson, Robert W. Dean, Alexander Alexiev, *East European Military Establishments: The Warsaw Pact Northern Tier*, RAND R-2417/1-AF/FF, December 1980.

28. Jan B. de Weydenthal, "The Catholic Church's Influence Grows in Poland," *RFE Research*, 30 October 1980.

29. Guetta from Warsaw in *Le Monde*, 4 Feburary 1981.

30. *Le Monde*, 20 and 21 February 1981.

31. Jan B. de Weydentahl, "The Problems of Power in Poland," *RFE Research*, 22 January 1981.

32. Cam Hudson, "Polish Reformers Inspired by Hungarian Model," *RFE Research*, 22 January 1981.

33. Bruce Porter, "Soviet Diplomacy towards Poland since the Gdańsk Accords," *Radio Liberty Research*, 4 December 1980 (*Radio Liberty Research Bulletin*, 12 December 1980.)

34. Willis from Riga, "Latvians Eye Polish 'Reforms' with Envy," *Christian Science Monitor*, 30 September 1980.

35. Alexander Alexiev, A. Ross Johnson, and S. Enders Wimbush, *If the Soviets Invade Poland*, RAND P-6569, December 1980.

Chapter 7

1. Quoted from Firuz Kazemzadeh, "Afghanistan: The Imperail Dream," *The New York Review of Books*, 21 Feburary 1980.

2. Karl Kaiser, "American-European Relations after the Afghanistan Crisis," testimony before the Subcommittee on Europe and the Middle East of

the House of Representatives Committee on International Relations, 22 September 1980; Dominique Moisi, "Les nouveaux malentendus transatlantiques" (paper delivered at a conference of the Institut québecois des relations internationales, Québec, P.Q., 26 September 1980); Uwe Nerlich, "Change in Europe: A Secular Trend?," *Daedalus* (Winter 1981); and "Push Comes to Shove," *The Economist*, 3 January 1981.

3. William E. Griffith, "The West German–American Relationship. The Threat of Deterioration," *Washington Quarterly* (Summer 1979).

4. Walter Laqueur, "Euro-Neutralism," *Commentary* (June 1980); and Laqueur, "Containment for the 1980s," *Commentary* October 1980.

5. Cf. the joint study by the foreign policy institutes in Bonn, New York, Paris, and London: Karl Kaiser, Winston Lord, Thierry de Montbrial, and David Watt, *Western Security: What Has Changed? What Should Be Done?* (New York: Council on Foreign Relations, 1981.)

Index

ABMs (antiballistic missiles), 18; treaty, 26
Adenauer, 14, 35, 37
Afghanistan, 10, 14, 16, 17, 18, 19, 26, 29, 31, 32, 36, 38, 39, 43, 55, 58, 65, 76, 78, 79, 81, 100, 101, 103, 106, 108
Albania, 15, 72, 74
Algeria, 66
"Alienation of affluence," 13, 14
AMaRV (advanced maneuvering reentry vehicle), 21
Angola, 10, 14, 18
Antisemitism, 86, 87
Arab-Israeli relations, 57; Camp David agreement, 58, 106, 110; Egyptian-Israeli peace treaty, 66; Middle East War (1967), 4, 12, 69, 70; Middle East War (1973), 13, 20, 58, 59, 61; Palestinian issue, 9, 35, 104, 107, 108, 109
"Arc of crisis," 8, 32
Arms control, 9, 10–11, 16–19, 20, 21, 24–26, 29–30, 43–52 *passim,* 55, 56, 78, 101, 104. *See also* LRTNF; M(B)FR; SALT
Arms sales, 37, 65
Asad, 58
ASALM (advanced strategic air-launched cruise missile), 21
ASW (anti-submarine warfare), 21, 25
Australia, 76
Austria, 45, 60
Automobile industry, 58–59
Autonomism, 76, 77, 78, 79

Babiuch, 90, 92
Backfire bombers, 27–28, 48, 52
Bahro, Rudolf, 34, 73
Balance of payments, 59–60, 62, 63
Baltic states, 3, 69, 100
Barczikowski, 90, 92, 99
Belgium, 9, 54, 56
Belgrade conference (1977), 41, 42–43
Benelux countries, 37, 45, 60, 104
Berlinguer, 78, 79
Biermann, Wolf, 34, 73
Birth rates, 2
BMD (ballistic missile defense), 21
Brandt, Willy, 33, 34, 36, 37, 40, 54, 55, 78, 80, 109
Bratkowski, Stefan, 93, 95
Brazil, 35, 76
Brezhnev, 3, 67, 79; and arms control, 43, 46, 53, 54, 55, 56; and détente, 1, 10, 32; and Poland, 84, 93, 96, 97, 100, 101
Bulgaria, 41, 72

Burt, Richard, 24–25
Bydgoszcz "provocation," 92, 94, 95, 97, 98

Cambodia, 15
Camp David agreements, 58, 106, 110
Carrillo, 73, 79
Carter, 5, 6; and détente, 10, 32; and human rights, 42, 71, 72; and Middle East oil, 58, 62; and nuclear arms, 22, 26, 29, 32, 53; and Schmidt, 35, 107; and USSR, 36, 55, 109
Catholic Church, 38, 54, 69, 71, 85–87; in Poland, 83–102 *passim*
CBMs (confidence-building measures), 42, 43, 44, 46
CDE (French conventional-disarmament proposal), 43, 53, 54–55
CDU (German Christian Democratic Party), 33, 37, 52, 54
CDU/CSU, 34, 35, 36, 37, 39, 53
Censorship, 92, 93, 95, 97, 100–101
Centrism, 98, 99
CEP (circular error of probability), 19–20
Chile, 37, 71
China: and Eurocommunism, 15, 77–78; and Indochina (Vietnam), 4, 15–16; and U.S., 14–15, 35, 40, 65, 77, 78, 100, 101; and USSR, 4–5, 9, 10, 11, 14–16, 33, 45, 48, 56, 71, 77–78, 83, 100, 101, 104, 108; and Yugoslavia, 15, 73
Christian Democrats (El Salvador), 37
Christian Democrats (Italy), 76, 77, 80, 81
Christian Democrats (Poland), 84, 88, 94
C^3I (command, control, communication, and intelligence systems), 19, 21, 26
CMs (cruise missiles), 19, 20, 25, 28, 32, 48, 49, 53, 54
Comecon countries, 60, 64, 65, 96
Communist ideology: Poland, 89–90; revisionism, 15, 73, 78, 86–87, 88, 89, 98, 101; USSR, 4, 5, 10–11, 12, 67, 71, 72, 75, 76, 77, 79. *See also* Eurocommunism
Conservatism, 1, 9, 81; U.S., 7–8, 18, 61; USSR, 3
"Correlation of forces," 10, 23, 57
Corruption, 85, 87
Cost-effectiveness (weaponry), 20, 21, 51
CPSU (Communist Party of the Soviet Union), 54; and Eurocommunism, 75–80
Craxi, 80
Credits, 64; Poland, 84, 85, 96, 97, 99, 101
Crisis management, 10, 13
Croatia, 74

About the Author

William E. Griffith is Ford Professor of Political Science at the Massachusetts Institute of Technology and Adjunct Professor of Diplomatic History at the Fletcher School of Law and Diplomacy, Tufts University. He is the author of many books, including three on Sino-Soviet relations and, most recently, *The Ostpolitik of the Federal Republic of Germany*. In 1981 he was a visiting professor of politics at the University of Munich. He has been a consultant to the National Security Council since 1977.